TIMEF

HORSES TO FOLLOW
2017/18 JUMPS SEASON

CONTENTS

TIMEFORM'S FIFTY TO FOLLOW 2017/18	**3**
HORSES TO FOLLOW FROM IRELAND	**47**
LOOKING AHEAD	**59**
Talking To The Trainers	60
Rising Stars	65
Ante-Post Betting	69
Leading Jumps Sires	76
REVIEW OF 2016/17	**79**
Timeform's View	80
Timeform's Best Of 2016/17	107
2016/17 Statistics	114
REFERENCE & INDEX	**115**
The Timeform Top 100	116
Promising Horses	118
Trainers For Courses	120
Index	135

TIMEF(O)RM

ISBN 978-0-9933900-8-1   Price £9.95

Printed and bound by
Charlesworth Press,
Wakefield, UK 01924 204830

SECTION

Timeform's Fifty To Follow, carefully chosen by members of Timeform's editorial staff, are listed below with their respective page numbers. A selection of ten (**marked in bold with a** ★) is made for those who prefer a smaller list.

ACTING LASS (IRE)	4	MINELLA AWARDS (IRE)	25
AMERICAN (FR) ★	5	MINELLA SUITE (IRE)	26
BARNEY DWAN (IRE)	6	MOLLY THE DOLLY (IRE)	27
BELAMI DES PICTONS (FR)	7	MONBEG AQUADUDE (IRE)	28
BENEAGLES (IRE)	8	**MOUNT MEWS (IRE)** ★	28
BILLY BRONCO	8	MR BIG SHOT (IRE)	30
BLACK OP (IRE)	9	NO HASSLE HOFF (IRE)	30
BOB FORD (IRE)	10	NOT ANOTHER MUDDLE	31
BRIO CONTI (FR) ★	10	OVERTOWN EXPRESS (IRE)	32
BURTONS WELL (IRE)	11	OXWICH BAY (IRE)	33
CALL ME LORD (FR) ★	12	PINGSHOU (IRE)	33
CAPTAIN FOREZ (FR) ★	13	POBBLES BAY (IRE)	34
CELEBRE D'ALLEN (FR)	13	POETIC RHYTHM (IRE)	35
CLAIMANTAKINFORGAN (FR)	14	POTTERS LEGEND	36
CONSTANTINE BAY	15	SAM'S ADVENTURE	37
COPAIN DE CLASSE (FR)	16	SAM SPINNER	38
DAPHNE DU CLOS (IRE) ★	16	SHIVERMETIMBERS	38
DEFI DU SEUIL (FR) ★	17	SINGLEFARMPAYMENT	39
DIABLE DE SIVOLA	19	SNOW LEOPARDESS	39
ELGIN	19	THOMAS CAMPBELL	40
FINIAN'S OSCAR (IRE) ★	20	TOPOFTHEGAME (IRE)	41
FORZA MILAN (IRE)	22	UNCLE ALASTAIR	42
IF THE CAP FITS (IRE) ★	22	WILLIE BOY (IRE)	43
IMPULSIVE STAR (IRE)	23	**WILLOUGHBY COURT (IRE)** ★	43
JUST MINDED (IRE)	24	YALA ENKI (FR)	45

The form summary for each horse is shown after its age, colour, sex and pedigree. The summary shows the distance, the state of the going and where the horse finished in each of its races since the start of the 2016/17 season. Performances are in chronological sequence with the date of its last race shown at the end (F–ran on Flat).

The distance of each race is given in furlongs. Steeplechase form figures are prefixed by the letter 'c', hurdle form figures by the letter 'h' and NH Flat race or bumper form figures by the letter 'b'.

The going is symbolised as follows: f–firm, m–good to firm; g–good, d–good to soft; s–soft; v–heavy.

Placings are indicated, up to the sixth place, by use of superior figures, an asterisk being used to denote a win and superior letters are used to convey what happened to a horse during the race: F–fell, pu–pulled up, ur–unseated rider, bd–brought down, su–slipped up, ro–ran out.

The Timeform Rating of a horse is simply the merit of the horse expressed in pounds and is arrived at by careful examination of its running against other horses. The ratings range from 175+ for the champions down to a figure of around 55 for selling platers. Symbols attached to the ratings: 'p'–likely to improve; 'P'–capable of much better form; '+'–the horse may be better than we have rated it.

Acting Lass (Ire) h133
6 b.g King's Theatre (Ire) – Darrens Lass (Ire) (Montelimar (USA))
2016/17 h19.7s* h21.7s² h19.3s⁴ Feb 18

Acting Lass must go into the same category as the likes of his fellow gelding Amy Blair, having a name that will confuse and catch out presenters, reporters, and punters alike. However she—sorry—he has plenty to recommend him on in terms of his form last season, which began with an impressive debut win at Hereford in November, where he settled things in a matter of strides leaving the back straight and stretched eleven lengths clear of his nearest pursuer on the run to the line. The impressive nature of this winning debut saw Acting Lass sent off at odds-on for his next start, where he was attempting to concede a penalty to £250,000 Irish point purchase Finian's Oscar, who was making his Rules debut. In hindsight, giving 6 lb to a horse who won the Grade 1 Tolworth Hurdle just nineteen days after and went on to also take the Mersey Novices' Hurdle later on in the season was a tough ask to say the least for Acting Lass, but he acquitted himself well, finishing second and leaving the third—a next-time-out winner—behind by ten lengths. That good effort had come over an extended two and a half miles and Acting Lass failed to match that level of form on his final start of the season, which came eight weeks later in a novice at Ascot. Out of a three-mile chaser who is a half-sister to Elzahaan, a winning chaser over twenty-seven furlongs, Acting Lass was perhaps unsurprisingly found a little wanting for pace in a steadily-run race over a shorter trip at Ascot, and he is better judged on his previous form. He should stay three miles when the time comes and is an exciting prospect for novice chasing this season. **Harry Fry**

Conclusion: *Second to Finian's Oscar in December reads particularly well and should have plenty more to offer when faced with longer trips and fences this season*

 # American (Fr) ★ | c156p
7 b.g Malinas (Ger) – Grande Sultane (Fr) (Garde Royale)
2016/17 c24.2s* c24s* c24s* Mar 18

American kept a lower profile than some of the big novice chasing names last season, running just three times and avoiding the main spring Festivals due to quick ground (said by his trainer to be fragile), but his achievements in the three races he won mark him down as a very interesting second-season chaser this term. His three wins all came over three miles on soft ground, starting with a novice chase at Exeter in November where he beat Label des Obeaux (who ended last season by winning a valuable Ayr handicap chase off a mark of 148) by two and a quarter lengths. On the face of it his next start—in the listed Hampton Novices' Chase at Warwick in January—fell apart somewhat, with market rivals Champers On Ice and Mystical Knight below their best, but it was hard not to be impressed with the way American gradually took each of his six rivals out of their comfort zone with a superbly accurate round of jumping and an injection of pace after halfway. He was briefly closed down at the last fence but highlighted his stamina by pulling out extra up the run-in, and he was a shorter price (8/1) for the National Hunt Chase over four miles than he was for the RSA Chase (12/1) over three miles in the Cheltenham Festival ante-post markets. The ground was deemed too quick for American at Cheltenham but he did run that week, in a novices' handicap chase on Uttoxeter's Midlands Grand National card, and he enhanced his reputation again, impressing by travelling strongly and jumping boldly. These particular attributes—along with his preference for soft ground—mark him down as a big contender for the likes of the Ladbrokes Gold Cup (formerly the Hennessy) at Newbury in December or the Welsh Grand National later that month. **Harry Fry**

Conclusion: *Unbeaten in three novice chase starts last season and impressed with his strong travelling, bold-jumping style; should have more to offer this season on soft ground*

The luckless Barney Dwan unseats jockey Paddy Brennan at Warwick

Barney Dwan (Ire)   h145 c138p

7 b.g Vinnie Roe (Ire) – Kapricia Speed (Fr) (Vertical Speed (Fr))
2016/17 c24g^2 c20.2d^{bd} h26s^{ur} h23.1s^4 h24g^2 h24.7g Apr 8

Barney Dwan must go down as one of the unluckiest horses in training from last season, and it is quite amazing that he didn't get his head in front on at least one occasion. He did everything bar win on his chasing debut at Kempton in November, really impressing with his jumping prior to slithering on landing and all but coming down at the last when around three lengths to the good. The fortuitous winner Potters Legend, another member of this year's *Fifty* who went on to finish fourth in the Kim Muir at the Cheltenham Festival, would have likely been beaten by more than three lengths had Barney Dwan not made that chance-ending mistake. As it turned out, though, Barney Dwan's hardships didn't end there. On his next start at Wincanton he was less than a length down and going well when brought down two out, looking a likely winner at the time. After his chasing misfortune his connections decided to revert to hurdles (perhaps with a mind to protecting his novice status over fences ahead of this season), but his luck did not improve on his first try back in that sphere at Warwick, as he was set for a good second to Tobefair when unseating his rider at the last. Things went more Barney Dwan's way for his final three starts of the campaign but he was contesting red-hot handicaps, and despite posting a career-best in the Pertemps Final at Cheltenham, he could not register a first win of the season, finishing second to the thrown-in Presenting Percy. A novice chase will be his for the taking this season when he goes back over fences, and given the round of jumping he put in at Kempton on his first chasing start last season, he may well end up bettering his smart hurdling form with a little more luck over the larger obstacles. *Fergal O'Brien*

Conclusion: *Had a luckless time of things last season but this smart hurdler has his novice status still intact and is expected to win races over fences this season; stays 3m*

Belami des Pictons (Fr)   c148p
6 b.g Khalkevi (Ire) – Nina des Pictons (Fr) (Denham Red (Fr))
2016/17 c21.1s⁴ c22.4d* c24v* c22.7s* Feb 28

Winner of five of his six starts since arriving in Britain and boasting an official BHA mark of 148, Belami des Pictons can hardly be classified as a dark horse, but he has the scope to make an even bigger breakthrough this season. Bought for €120,000 following a victory at Vichy, he won a pair of novice hurdles in March 2016 before making his chasing debut at Fontwell in November. Belami des Pictons finished well held that day, but showed the benefit of that experience when winning his next start (which came in a competitive novice handicap chase at Newbury on New Year's Eve), travelling well and seeing out the extended two miles and six furlongs strongly for a horse who had yet to turn six. He progressed again to take apart a small-field Warwick novices' chase six weeks later, relishing the heavy ground and putting up a smart performance to win by twenty-two lengths. Belami des Pictons was clearly held in high regard by his shrewd trainer, holding several entries for the Cheltenham Festival, including in the RSA Chase, but he did not run at all in the spring, and was last seen when easily dispatching the useful Zeroeshadesofgrey in a match at Leicester at the end of February.

Connections' patience in skipping the big spring festivals may well pay dividends this season, and it would be no surprise to see Belami des Pictons head for a valuable handicap chase this winter, perhaps even the Ladbrokes Gold Cup (formerly known as the Hennessy)—a race that has twice been won by a six-year-old in the past four years. *Venetia Williams*

Conclusion: *Lightly-raced chaser who looks sure to win some valuable prizes when the mud is flying this winter; has the potential to make up into a graded performer in time*

Beneagles (Ire) h126p

5 b.g Milan – Liss Rua (Ire) (Bob Back (USA))
2016/17 h19.9s^{pu} h24.5d^2 h21.2s^2 h25d* h23.5m^5 Apr 2

Beneagles, as any whisky enthusiast will know, shares his name with a brand of scotch, which at its prime was one of the most popular in Scotland during the 1970s. However, that particular brand is now defunct, meaning Alan King's runner is left to fly the flag on his own. Much like his liquid cousin, which can take a number of years to mature and produce a return, Beneagles required a certain level of patience during his first season as a racehorse, pulling up on his hurdling debut at Uttoxeter despite having gone off at a single-figure price.

Two fairly useful efforts to finish as runner-up in novice hurdles at Kempton and Ludlow followed, with the stronger of the two coming in the former, when Beneagles finished three quarters of a length behind the more experienced Ballymalin, who went on to run with credit in the Pertemps Final at the Cheltenham Festival later in the season. Like Ballymalin, Beneagles also relishes a test of stamina over hurdles, and he got off the mark at the fourth attempt when upped to beyond three miles in a match race at Huntingdon in March.

Beneagles was handed an opening BHA mark of 127, and took in his first handicap at Ascot in April. Despite the race being run over three miles, it was a relative test of speed on good to firm ground, and Beneagles was not seen to best effect. His opening handicap mark is likely to prove workable under a more suitable set of circumstances, however, and he remains open to further improvement this season over hurdles, while as a useful-looking ex-Irish pointer, he will surely have a future over fences at some stage. *Alan King*

Conclusion: *Showed plenty of potential during his opening season over hurdles and his current BHA mark is likely to prove workable when he gets a suitable test of stamina over 3m+*

Billy Bronco h118+

6 ch.g Central Park (Ire) – Nan (Buckley)
2016/17 h18.9v^3 h21.9v^2 h24.3v* h21.5s^4 Mar 10

One of the more heart-warming stories to emerge from last season's National Hunt campaign was that of Tobefair, a horse trained by Pembrokeshire-based Debra Hamer and owned by a syndicate based at the local Cresselly Arms, who completed a remarkable seven-timer when winning a handicap at Newbury in February from a mark 53 lb higher than when his winning streak had started at Worcester in 2015.

Though he couldn't make it eight wins in a row when pitched in to the Pertemps Final at last season's Cheltenham Festival, Tobefair is the stuff of syndicate dreams, and we are hoping that his full-brother Billy Bronco can take off in the same way this season. Billy Bronco also started life with Debra Hamer, but was sold to Evan Williams and William and Angela Rucker for £110,000 after winning a Towcester bumper on debut in January 2016. Billy Bronco had looked suited by the emphasis on stamina that day on heavy ground, and was immediately stepped up in trip by Williams, finishing third at Haydock on his hurdling debut over two and a quarter miles before pulling eighteen lengths clear of the third when second to Ballymalin (who went on to win next time out and then finish fifth in the Sefton Novices' Hurdle at Aintree) over two and three quarter miles at Ffos Las in December. There was an element of fortune involved when Billy Bronco went one better on his next outing, benefitting from the fall of the long-time leader in a maiden hurdle at Ayr, but his Ffos Las second has a solid look to it and there are races to be won with him over staying trips this season from a BHA mark in the low 120s. **Evan Williams**

Conclusion: *Brother to winning machine Tobefair who could also take off this season when the emphasis is on stamina; remains unexposed after only one handicap start*

Black Op (Ire)   b111
6 br.g Sandmason – Afar Story (Ire) (Desert Story (Ire))
2016/17 b16.6g* b17g Apr 7

You could probably be forgiven for not knowing that Sir Henry Cecil's 2001 Hardwicke Stakes winner Sandmason had a career as a National Hunt sire, given how few of his progeny have made an impact on the racecourse to date (highest Timeform rating achieved by the best of his National Hunt runners is just 118). Some of his offspring clearly look the part, however, and have taken the eye of powerful owner Roger Brookhouse, who paid £210,000 for wide-margin Irish point winner Black Op at the Goffs UK Aintree sale in April 2016, and £130,000 for bumper winner Summerville Boy at the Goffs UK Spring sale in May 2017. A year on from being sold at the track, Black Op was sent off a well-backed 100/30 favourite for the Grade 2 bumper at Aintree's Grand National meeting, though he ran below the form of his debut bumper win at Doncaster, where he'd beaten another member of this year's *Fifty* Claimantakinforgan (fifth at Aintree) by two and a half lengths. Claimantakinforgan had finished third in Cheltenham's Champion Bumper prior to his run at Aintree, and the form of Black Op's win has a particularly solid look to it given that the time compared very favourably with both of the two-mile hurdles races that had taken place earlier on the card. A rangy sort with plenty of ability, he is an exciting prospect for novice hurdles this season and is certainly bred for the job on his dam's side, with the likes of Balthazar King in the family. **Tom George**

Conclusion: *Expensive purchase after wide-margin win in Irish point who won a good-looking bumper at Doncaster on Rules debut in February; exciting prospect*

Bob Ford (Ire)   c121§
10 b.g Vinnie Roe (Ire) – Polar Lamb (Ire) (Brush Aside (USA))
2016/17 h23.9g⁴ c25.5d c29.2s^pu c23.8s⁴ c23.8v^pu Mar 19

The veterans' chase initiative that was introduced by the BHA in 2014/15 to create more opportunities for chasers aged ten and above has been a roaring success in the past couple of seasons, with old favourites competing for big prizes across the eleven-race series, which culminates in a final on Tolworth Hurdle day at Sandown in January.

Dr Richard Newland knows the time of day, and may well have some of these valuable prizes in mind for one of his newer (yet older) recruits, Bob Ford, who joins the yard as a well-handicapped ten-year-old, purchased for just £7,000 out of the Rebecca Curtis yard in March. Bob Ford was rated as high as 141 by the BHA at his peak for Curtis, a mark he was allocated after winning the brutal 2015 West Wales National at Ffos Las by ninety-eight lengths from the only other finisher. Bob Ford clearly has extreme reserves of stamina, the only member of the field to handle the conditions that day, and it isn't surprising that his most recent victory also came on heavy ground at the same track, this time from a BHA mark of 133. He has joined a yard well adept at rejuvenating horses who have lost their way and has dropped to a BHA mark of 122—his lowest since his very first handicap win at Chepstow in 2014—so although his recent form figures leave plenty to be desired, he can hopefully pick up a race or two this winter when the mud is flying and the emphasis is very much on stamina. A heavy ground veterans' race over three miles, a contest likely to be plentiful in prize money and short in unexposed sorts, is perhaps something his shrewd new handler will have in mind as a potential target. **Dr Richard Newland**

Conclusion: *Hard to catch right for former yard so has to be one of this year's riskier propositions, but is on a good mark and has joined a trainer renowned for getting horses back on track*

Brio Conti (Fr) ★   h140p
6 gr.g Dom Alco (Fr) – Cadoulie Wood (Fr) (Cadoudal (Fr))
2016/17 b16.3g* h16.2d^F h18.9v² h16.8g h19.4g* h21g* h20g⁵ Apr 8

Brio Conti made it into last year's *Fifty* as a novice hurdler after making a good impression in bumpers, and though he failed to win on his first three starts over hurdles last season—including when falling on his debut at Kelso—he went on to justify his inclusion by winning twice in early-2017. Brio Conti eventually put it all together on his fourth start when winning a novice over hurdles at Doncaster in January by nine lengths, and with the form of that race looking strong (next-time-out winners in second and fifth), Brio Conti was one of Paul Nicholls' main Cheltenham Festival hopes, being entered in the Martin Pipe. He narrowly missed the cut for that race in the end, but would probably have won it given the manner of his victory in Kempton's Silver Plate (a Festival consolation race) a few days later. It is rare to see a horse stand out as much as Brio Conti did in such a competitive handicap, going through the race powerfully and still being on the bridle long after everything else was flat to the boards. The impression he created led to him being sent off at just 5/1 for his next start in the Grade 1 Mersey Novices' Hurdle at Aintree, and he wasn't at all disgraced in a much stronger race, beaten just over eight lengths into fifth by Finian's Oscar. John Hales, who part-owns Brio Conti under the Gi Gi Syndicate, has had some top-class chasers over the years and Brio Conti looks another smart novice chasing prospect this term, with races like the JLT at the Cheltenham Festival likely be top of his agenda. **Paul Nicholls**

Conclusion: *Useful form in hurdles last season but could make up into an even better chaser given his pedigree and physique; travels strongly and all of his wins have come on good ground*

Burtons Well (Ire) c137p

8 b.g Well Chosen – Despute (Ire) (Be My Native (USA))
2016/17 c16.4s² c20v* c20.8s⁴ c20.4gᶠ Mar 14

Burton Port only met with defeat once over fences during his novice campaign in 2009/10, that coming in the RSA Chase at the Cheltenham Festival, and given how prolific he was during that season it is surprising that he went without a win for the rest of his career, despite having raced a further sixteen times. Though he didn't manage another win, Burton Port produced his best performances on Timeform ratings after his novice season, finishing second in the 2010 Hennessy Gold Cup and fourth in the 2012 Cheltenham Gold Cup, and we are hoping that his half-brother Burtons Well, who wears the same silks of owner Trevor Hemmings, can go on improving during his second term over fences—and hopefully add to his win tally in the process.

Burtons Well must have had a problem to be off the track for twenty-one months between his final novice hurdle start and his first start over fences, but he was strong in the betting on his belated return at Sedgefield in November and shaped well in second behind the promising Waiting Patiently, a member of last season's *Fifty* who went on to win a Grade 2 at Haydock in January. Burtons Well went one better when upped to two and a half miles at Uttoxeter in December despite taking a strong hold, and was subsequently sent off at 15/2 for a warm novice handicap chase at Cheltenham on Festival Trials Day. Burtons Well was matched at 2.6 in-running on the Betfair Exchange before weakening approaching the final fence, shaping much better than the bare result (crossed the line in fourth, beaten nearly twenty lengths). It was too early to tell whether Burtons Well would have seen things out a little better on his next start in the Close Brothers Novices' Chase at the Cheltenham Festival, but he was going smoothly through the race when he fell at the ninth (after being gambled on) and he looks well worth another chance to make a mark in the high-130s look lenient.

Venetia Williams

Conclusion: *Plenty of promise shown as a novice over fences and looks capable of landing a couple of handicaps this season*

Call Me Lord (Fr) ★   h142p
4 b.g Slickly (Fr) – Sosa (Ger) (Cape Cross (Ire))
2016/17 h16.4d⁵ h16.4s* h17.9v* h16g* Apr 29

The juvenile handicap hurdle on Sandown's Jumps Finale card at the end of April was run for the first time in 2012 and has already produced some notable graded hurdlers, including 2013 winner Ptit Zig (who won the Group 1 Grande Course de Haies d'Auteuil Hurdle in 2016) and 2015 winner Lil Rockerfeller (second in last season's Stayers' Hurdle at the Cheltenham Festival). The latest winner Call Me Lord has the potential to make up into that sort of animal, too, with the performance he put in to win the race on his stable/British debut bettered by few others among the crop of four-year-old hurdlers last season.

The first of Call Me Lord's two wins in the French Provinces for former trainer Mickael Seror came in remarkable fashion given that he'd jumped badly right throughout before coming from a seemingly impossible position to lead on the line, and he did plenty wrong in the jumping department again at Sandown, hurdling none too fluently and making a notable error at the last, but still winning by three and three quarter lengths from Dolos. His jumping may well have been addressed by his new yard over the summer, however, and the fact that he was still able to defy top weight from an opening BHA mark of 135 despite such a poor round of jumping and having been trapped in a pocket turning for home was impressive in itself, while it was hard not to be taken with the powerful manner in which he travelled through the race under Daryl Jacob. He has been raised 8 lb in the handicap for that win, but he is an exciting prospect with a lot of untapped potential, and he could prove better than a handicapper if becoming more fluent at his hurdles. **Nicky Henderson**

Conclusion: *Created an excellent impression when winning a juvenile handicap on British/yard debut at the end of last season despite doing plenty wrong in the race; a hurdler with lots of untapped potential who could make up into a graded performer in time*

Captain Forez (Fr) ★   h144p

5 b.g Network (Ger) – Pourkoipa du Forez (Fr) (Robin des Champs (Fr))
2016/17 h16.3d³ h15.7d² h20g² Apr 8

Grand National-winning owner John Hales has primarily based his horses with Paul Nicholls in recent years, though Alan King, Nicky Richards and Donald McCain have also trained for him within the last ten seasons. Dan Skelton—formerly Nicholls' assistant—has also had a few sent to him, though in the cases of Mac's Return, Fascino Rustico and Al Ferof they were horses who had previously lost their form for Nicholls. After returning the latter pair to winning ways, Skelton is now taking a more primary role in the training of Hales' horses, and Captain Forez became the first of the owner's stock to start life in Britain with Skelton. Captain Forez won't be the last to do that, either, with Hales' recent big-money buys Maire Banrigh and The Dellercheckout reportedly being split between Skelton and Nicholls.

That pair were both Irish point winners and, like many of Hales' buys, chasing is likely to be the primary focus. That also goes for Captain Forez, a well-made chasing sort on looks, though after going without a win during his novice hurdling campaign last season, he isn't guaranteed to make the switch to fences immediately this term. Though he didn't manage to win a race, Captain Forez ended last season with a lofty rating over hurdles, having found only Finian's Oscar too good in the Grade 1 Mersey Novices' Hurdle at Aintree in April. He looked to benefit from the step up to two and a half miles that day and will stay further still. Options are wide-ranging for him this season but a maiden win over hurdles would be a formality, while he is likely to make a smashing staying chaser when the time comes. ***Dan Skelton***

Conclusion: *Without a win over hurdles last season but excellent second to Finian's Oscar at Aintree means that a maiden will be his for the taking if connections fancy, while he should prove even better when going chasing*

Celebre d'Allen (Fr)   b100+

5 ch.g Network (Ger) – Revoltee (Fr) (Grand Seigneur (Fr))
2016/17 b16.7d³ b15.3v³ Feb 2

Allan Stennett has placed his horses with a number of different yards during his time as an owner, but recent success in his beige and green checked colours has come courtesy of David Pipe, and in one race at the Cheltenham Festival in particular, the race most recently known as the Brown Advisory and Merriebelle Stable Plate. Salut Flo landed a gamble with ease when winning the race in 2012, and though Ballynagour failed to justify 7/2 favouritism one year on for the same connections, he returned with a vengeance in 2014, winning the race by eight lengths. Stennett, Pipe and Tom Scudamore went agonisingly close to landing an unprecedented third Plate in four seasons when Monetaire was narrowly touched off—after enduring a troubled passage—in the 2015 running of the race.

It may be a while before we see Celebre d'Allen in the Plate, but after showing plenty of promise in both his bumper starts last season, this £100,000 ex-pointer could easily progress into a Festival prospect. He went like the best horse at the weights on his Rules debut at Bangor in January, quickening clear two furlongs out before his inexperience and early exuberance told and he was collared in the final furlong by both Just A Sting and Fin And Game. Celebre d'Allen filled the same position on his second and final start last season a month later at Wincanton, again travelling powerfully and looking the winner, but being unable to quicken in gruelling conditions. The form from those bumpers is stacking up, with both winners going on to defy penalties and Wincanton second Lalor winning the Grade 2 bumper at Aintree, and a regulation bumper will be Celebre d'Allen's for the taking should he be persevered with in that sphere, though big-field handicaps over jumps are where he is likely to come into his own. *David Pipe*

Conclusion: *Showed plenty of promise in a pair of bumpers that have worked out well and looks a good prospect for big-field handicaps over jumps*

Claimantakinforgan (Fr)   b115

5 b.g Great Pretender (Ire) – Taquine d'Estrees (Fr) (Take Risks (Fr))
2016/17 b15.7v* b15.7d⁶ b16.6g² b16.4g³ b17g⁵ Apr 7

Owners Mike Grech and Stuart Parkin are relatively new patrons of racing but their band of mainly ex-Irish point winners have quickly made an impact at the very highest level, with three of their runners making the frame in races at last season's Cheltenham Festival. River Wylde finished third in the Supreme and Constantine Bay—another of this year's *Fifty*—was fourth in the Albert Bartlett, but the closest they came to a first Festival winner, and indeed a first Grade 1 winner, was when Claimantakinforgan finished third in the Champion Bumper, just two and three quarter lengths behind Fayonagh.

Purchased for £110,000 after winning his second start in points (beating Lough Derg Spirit, another subsequent Grech and Parkin purchase, into third) Claimantakinforgan seemed to relish the emphasis on stamina when getting off the mark at the first time of asking under Rules in a heavy-ground bumper at Haydock in November, looking as though he'd be well suited by tackling further than two miles. He was considered for a novice hurdling campaign after his win, but was kept to bumpers for the rest of the season (presumably to avoid clashes with his owners' other runners, the majority of which were novice hurdlers) where he showed smart form, not only placing in the Champion Bumper at Cheltenham but also chasing home Black Op (another member of this year's *Fifty*) in a good time whilst giving weight away at Doncaster in February. A strike-rate of one from five makes Claimantakinforgan's profile slightly less eye-catching than some of last season's bumper horses, but only a few will have run to a bigger rating and he remains with bags of potential with a view to longer trips. **Nicky Henderson**

Conclusion: *Smart bumper performer who should have plenty more to offer when going beyond 2m over hurdles this season*

Constantine Bay   h144

6 b.g Kayf Tara – Alina Rheinberg (Ger) (Waky Nao)
2016/17 h18.9v* h19.5s* h24.4d* h24g⁴ h24.7g⁴ Apr 7

The Albert Bartlett often proves to be one of the most gruelling races of the entire Cheltenham Festival, with the usual scenario involving a big field and strong pace which, combined with a stiff track, provides a test that many of the novices involved have yet to face. This was not the case in the latest renewal, however, which was run at a muddling pace and didn't test stamina to the same extent that it usually does. This put paid to the chances of 13/8-favourite Death Duty, who raced freely and was beaten when he unseated his jockey at the last, and the tactical nature of the race would have also been of no use to Constantine Bay, who had won the River Don at Doncaster over an extended three miles in determined fashion on his previous start. Constantine Bay would probably have still made the places, however, but for being stopped in his tracks two flights from home after the fall of The Worlds End, and he did well to pick himself back up and eventually finish fourth. Constantine Bay was possibly still feeling the effects of that race when he lined up three weeks later in the Sefton Novices' Hurdle at Aintree, lacking much fluency all round, but with stamina as a strong suit and the looks/background to make a smashing chaser, he is one of the best prospects to take out of both races going forward, and the National Hunt Chase at this season's Festival could be right up his street given the stamina reserves he has shown. **Nicky Henderson**

Conclusion: *Not seen to best effect in last season's muddling Albert Bartlett and looks the sort to relish a stamina test over fences this season*

Copain de Classe (Fr)   h132p

5 b.g Enrique – Toque Rouge (Fr) (Loup Solitaire (USA))
2016/17 h19.5d³ h16d* h19.8vᵖᵘ h15.3d* Mar 26

"In a move which will surprise the racing world, Paul Nicholls has turned to his two former assistants Dan Skelton and Harry Fry to increase his chances of becoming champion trainer for a tenth time."

Those words were part of an article that appeared on the betting.betfair.com website on the first morning of the month of April in 2016, and Nicholls did win the Trainers Championship referred to that season without the need of any 'outside assistance' (check the date). Horses from the Skelton and Fry yards are again well represented in this year's *Fifty*, but their former 'gaffer' continues to show no signs of slowing down, even if the champion trainer title passed back to Nicky Henderson on the final day of the most recent campaign.

Copain de Classe did his bit for Nicholls' title campaign last season, winning two of his four starts, the first of which being at short odds in a novice hurdle over two miles at Chepstow in November. Copain de Class seemed unsuited by the testing conditions when pulled up on his next start over two and a half miles at Wincanton, but he got back on the up when beating seven rivals at the same track in another novice in late-March, jumping well and travelling strongly before easing clear of Azzuri (who has since made a promising start to his novice chasing career). It may be that the pair renew rivalry at some stage with Copain de Classe seemingly set to follow a similar path this season, and as a well-made sort he is one to look out for when meeting a fence. All three of his wins (including his bumper win in France) have come away from testing ground. ***Paul Nicholls***

Conclusion: *Not over-raced as a hurdler and looks a potentially smart recruit to the novice chasing ranks if switching disciplines as anticipated, likely to prove best at around 2m on going no worse than good to soft*

Daphne du Clos (Ire) ★   b109

4 b.f Spanish Moon (USA) – Katarina du Clos (Fr) (Panoramic)
2016/17 b11.9g* b14s² b16.3d* Feb 11

Cheltenham's Champion Bumper isn't a race favoured by every owner/trainer in racing given the test it poses to young horses who are still in development, and with only three runners in the previous five renewals, Nicky Henderson is presumably of the opinion that the race isn't suitable for many of his bumper horses. It may well be significant, then, that he was considering running a thrice-raced four-year-old filly in this year's renewal. Daphne du Clos had been second favourite for the Champion

Bumper until being ruled out with a "tiny" setback in the week leading up to the Festival, but she was likely to have played a big part based on her easy defeat of Western Ryder and Dans Le Vent, fifth and sixth at Cheltenham, in a listed bumper at Newbury in February. That Newbury bumper is traditionally the strongest race of its type before the major spring festivals; Ballyandy took the race in 2016 before following up in the Champion Bumper, while Grade 1 winning hurdler Barters Hill beat Champion Hurdler Buveur d'Air and Supreme/Arkle winner Altior in the 2015 renewal. Daphne du Clos' easy win in the 2017 renewal was her first in Britain (she'd won a French bumper on her debut), but she probably should have won her previous start for Henderson in a listed four-year-old bumper at Cheltenham on New Year's Day, having closed all the way to the line and been beaten just a head by Cap Soleil despite still showing signs of immaturity. She is expected to take high rank amongst the fillies/mares in novice events over hurdles this season, with the Jane Seymour Mares' Novices' Hurdle at Sandown (recently upgraded to Grade 2 status) in February and the Dawn Run Mares' Novices' Hurdle at the Cheltenham Festival two valuable potential targets. **Nicky Henderson**

Conclusion: *Easy winner of a traditionally strong Newbury bumper in February before missing the spring festivals with a small setback; a very interesting novice prospect this season and likely to take high rank amongst her own sex*

Defi du Seuil (Fr) ★   h151p

4 b.g. Voix du Nord (Fr) – Quarvine du Seuil (Fr) (Lavirco (Ger))
2016/17 b11.9s* h15.8d* h16.4s* h16.8d* h16s* h16.8s* h16.8g* h17g* Apr 6

After a flawless juvenile season in which he notched up a perfect seven wins out of seven, including three Grade 1s, Defi du Seuil is one of the more obvious inclusions in this year's *Fifty*, but a horse that remains with so much potential is hard to leave out. A private purchase from France after winning a Lyon bumper by seven and a half lengths in April 2016, Defi Du Seuil began his British career in a low-key Ffos Las juvenile maiden, but quickly graduated to better things, winning the Grade 2 Prestbury Hurdle at Cheltenham just four weeks later, having been well backed. Another victory at Cheltenham followed in mid-December before Defi du Seuil was upped to Grade 1 level for the first time in the Future Champions Finale Juvenile Hurdle at Chepstow, and he impressed with how quickly he settled matters in the straight, winning easily by thirteen lengths. Defi du Seuil certainly lived up to the title of that race, adding two more Grade 1s to his tally in the spring in the form of the Triumph at Cheltenham and the Anniversary Hurdle at Aintree.

It is notoriously hard for champion juveniles to make an impact at the highest level in the open division the following season (as fans of Peace And Co will know only too

Defi du Seuil clears away in the Triumph Hurdle

well), but Defi du Seuil very much appeals as the sort to train on, a lengthy National Hunt-bred who, unlike many other juveniles, hasn't come from the Flat. Defi du Seuil will have to improve plenty on what he has done as a four-year-old if he is to make up into a Champion Hurdle contender as his connections hope he may (current ante-post odds of around 8/1 for that race seem short), but he is a very exciting prospect for this season regardless. **Philip Hobbs**

Conclusion: *Last season's champion juvenile boasts a perfect record over hurdles and though he will have to improve to mix it at Grade 1 level in open company this term, he appeals as the type to train on and should have even more to offer*

Diable de Sivola h130

4 b.g. Noroit (Ger) – Grande Route (Ire) (Lost World (Ire))
2016/17 h15.8g* h17.7d² h15.8g³ h16.4s² h16.6g³ h16.4g⁵ Mar 15

Tea For Two's win in last season's Mildmay at Aintree was a second top-level success for him, but he still has some way to go to match the Nick Williams yard's main flag-bearer from recent years, Reve de Sivola, who was a six-time Grade 1 winner across a career spanning nine seasons. Like others sporting the 'Sivola' name, Reve de Sivola was bred by Gilles and Thomas Trapenard at Haras de Sivola stud in Lalizolle, France.

Diable de Sivola is a member of the current crop of Sivolas, and overcame a lack of experience when making a winning debut in a juvenile event at Uttoxeter last July. It was inexperience that proved his undoing at Fontwell two months later when second in a tactical affair, however, and he looked a hard ride when going right handed for the first time at Huntingdon in October. Diable de Sivola seemed to appreciate the return to a left-handed track and a switch to hold-up tactics when showing much improved form on his next start, in the Grade 2 Prestbury Hurdle at Cheltenham in November, strictly emerging best at the weights in finishing less than two lengths behind Defi du Seuil (though the winner was value for quite a bit more than the bare margin). Luckily, the handicapper didn't take that form literally, and Diable de Sivola was given an opening handicap mark of 132, which he ran off in the Fred Winter at the Cheltenham Festival. Diable de Sivola gave the impression that his opening mark will not prove beyond him another day, finishing with a rattle for fifth from an uncompromising position having suffered interference earlier in the race, and he is sure to have more to offer next term, just the sort his yard will continue to improve. **Nick Williams**

Conclusion: *Eye-catching fifth in the Fred Winter means there are likely to be races to be won with him from a BHA mark of 132 this season*

Elgin h143

5 b.g Duke of Marmalade (Ire) – China Tea (USA) (High Chaparral (Ire))
2016/17 b17d² h16.4s* h16g* h15.7s² h16g² h16.4g Mar 14

The Elite Racing Club enjoyed an excellent Flat season in 2017 with Marsha becoming their highest-rated Flat performer ever, running to a Timeform rating of 130 when winning the Nunthorpe at York. The club's highest-rated Flat horse before Marsha had been Soviet Song, who'd held that accolade since 2005, a season when she won the Falmouth and was second in the Sussex. Elite Racing have been waiting even longer for a new jumping superstar to emerge, with 1996 Stayers' Hurdle second Mysilv still their highest rated jumps performer, though that could change this season if Elgin continues his progression.

Elgin fell short of the very best novice hurdlers last season, having been well held in the Supreme at Cheltenham on his final start after being outclassed by Neptune second Neon Wolf in the Rossington Main at Haydock and then going down to Supreme third River Wylde in the Dovecote at Kempton, but he has the physical scope to progress further during his second season over obstacles. He is Flat-bred and has plenty of speed, which he showed when winning a warm-looking novice over two miles at Kempton on Boxing Day off a slow gallop. The favourite for that race, Jenkins, was disappointing, but Elgin gave 5 lb and a one and three quarter length beating to Dan Skelton's Mohaayed, who did best of those held up when third in the Scottish Champion Hurdle later in the season from a BHA mark of 135. Based on that Kempton form, Elgin would be of interest if sent handicapping this season from a mark of 140, with the likes of the Greatwood at Cheltenham and the Wessex Youth Trust Handicap Hurdle at Ascot appealing as suitable pre-Christmas targets. *Alan King*

Conclusion: *Fell short of the top 2m novice hurdlers last season but has the physical scope to improve further and looks to be on a workable handicap mark on the balance of his form*

Ben Fearnley, Content Editor (Elgin): *"The two-mile novice hurdle at Kempton on Boxing Day has been won by some serious horses in recent years, including Altior 2015, and though it is stretching it to think that Elgin will develop into quite that good a performer this season, he does look well handicapped on the bare form of his win in the 2016 renewal. Reportedly set to stay over hurdles this season, I'll be backing him for whichever top two-mile handicap he shows up in first."*

Finian's Oscar (Ire) ★   h150p

5 b.g. Oscar (Ire) – Trinity Alley (Ire) (Taipan (Ire))
2016/17 h21.7s* h16s* h16.8s* h20g* h20g² Apr 28

As racehorse names go, Finian's Oscar may not be the most original for a son of Oscar out of a half-sister to the 2012 Champion Chaser Finian's Rainbow, but there has been nothing underwhelming about the progress he has made since his eight-length point win at Portrush in late-October.

Finian's Oscar caught the eye of bloodstock agent Tom Malone and was purchased for £250,000 on behalf of Ann and Alan Potts. It wasn't long before Finian's Oscar was starting to repay his new owners, using a Hereford novice hurdle victory in mid-December as a stepping stone to the Grade 1 Tolworth Hurdle at Sandown less than three weeks later. Sent off at 11/10 for an event with a proud roll of honour, he

Finian's Oscar is expected to take high rank amongst the novice chasers this season

stamped his authority on the race in the straight, finishing with five lengths in hand of the more experienced Grade 2 winner Capitaine, a performance that catapulted him to the head of the betting for the Neptune, his expected Cheltenham Festival target. Finian's Oscar completed a simple task in a listed race at Exeter the following month, but any Cheltenham dreams were shattered when he suffered a setback in the week before the Festival.

Fortunately, this proved only a minor hitch as Finian's Oscar returned to land an above-average renewal of Aintree's Mersey Novices' Hurdle in April, and there was much anticipation when he travelled across the Irish Sea to take on three fellow Grade 1-winners in Punchestown's Champion Novices' Hurdle later that month. Finian's Oscar relinquished his unblemished record in agonising circumstances, seemingly in control early in the straight but collared near the finish by the fast-finishing Bacardys, but it is difficult to believe that there will not be more to come from him further down the line given what he has achieved in such a short space of time. Both his background between the flags and physique (rangy sort) point towards him taking high rank amongst the novice chasers this season. ***Colin Tizzard***

Conclusion: *A smart novice hurdler who looks an exciting prospect for 2017/18, particularly with chasing in mind*

 Follow us on Twitter @Timeform

Forza Milan (Ire)   h131
5 b.g Milan – Nonnetia (Fr) (Trempolino (USA))
2016/17 b16g[6] h20s[2] h19.6d[2] h19.5v* h23g[6] Sep 18

Forza Milan raced four times last season, once in a bumper and three times over hurdles, breaking his maiden tag on his final start in a two and a half mile maiden hurdle at Chepstow in late-February at 11/8. Though he did not race during the spring months, Forza Milan arguably became even more interesting as a jumping prospect, particularly after Aintree's Grand National meeting. Firstly, the horse that he had chased home on his penultimate start at Huntingdon, Rather Be, gained compensation for his unlucky exit in the Martin Pipe at Cheltenham by winning the twenty-two-runner Aintree equivalent. That was a nice boost to Forza Milan's form, but his connections would perhaps have been even more encouraged when they saw their horse's full-brother One For Arthur come from right out the back to win the National itself a day later by four and a half lengths. One For Arthur won three times over hurdles himself at trips of up to three miles before he was sent chasing, and there are further races to be won with Forza Milan in the same sphere, with an opening BHA mark of 128 likely to prove workable (shaped encouragingly on his handicap debut at Worcester in mid-September when easy to back). Time and distance are likely to prove Forza Milan's friends, so while he is expected to win further races this season when upped in trip, he is also a very interesting long-term chasing prospect. *Jonjo O'Neill*

Conclusion: *Full-brother to last year's Grand National hero One For Arthur who will be of plenty of interest when stepping up in trip to beyond 3m this season*

If The Cap Fits (Ire) ★   b115+
5 b.g. Milan – Derravaragh Sayra (Ire) (Sayarshan (Fr))
2016/17 b17.7g* b16.5g* b17g[4] Apr 7

Harry Fry, who was Paul Nicholls' assistant for four years, has made giant strides since he started training in 2012, each year increasing both his total number of winners and prize money, and breaking through the £1million barrier last season for the first time. Unowhatimeanharry, who made it into the 2015/16 edition of this publication, has been Fry's main money spinner, winning nine of his ten starts since joining the yard and earning almost £400,000 in prize money. If The Cap Fits has a long way to go to replicate Unowhatimeanharry's accomplishments, but he made an encouraging start in bumpers last season, and is an exciting hurdling prospect.

If The Cap Fits won two of his three starts in bumpers last season, which bodes particularly well given his stout pedigree (out of a half-sister to useful hurdler/chaser Duke of Lucca, who stays thirty-one furlongs). He was strong in the betting for his debut at Plumpton, and duly showed himself to be a good prospect, leading on the bridle until he was headed briefly in the home straight, but asserting under two furlongs out to win convincingly. As expected, he showed improved form to follow up under a penalty on his next start at Taunton three months later, winning by nine lengths and looking better the further he went. Although he lost his unbeaten record in the Grade 2 bumper at Aintree on his final start, he shaped as though he would have benefited from a stronger gallop, and is arguably as good a prospect for staying novice hurdles as any in that field. *Harry Fry*

Conclusion: *Smart bumper performer who is very stoutly bred; potential to make up into a leading novice hurdler this season once tackling 2½m+*

Impulsive Star (Ire)   h134p

7 b.g Busy Flight – Impulsive Ita (Ire) (Supreme Leader)
2016/17 h20s* h24s⁴ h25.3g* h23.1s* h24g Mar 16

The Pertemps Final has undergone a transformation in recent years, with the usual field of exposed and poorly handicapped stayers now replaced with lightly raced and

Impulsive Star wins at Exeter on handicap debut

progressive novices or second-season hurdlers. This is due in no small part to the rule changes made by the BHA in regard to qualification for the final, with runners for last season's race required to have finished in the top six in one of the qualifiers in Britain/ Ireland.

Impulsive Star had been one of the most impressive qualifier winners, and was sent off as 8/1 favourite for the final in a field of twenty-four. He very much fits the new build of Pertemps runners, his impressive qualifier win at Exeter in February had been his handicap debut, and had come just three months on from his first start in Britain when winning a maiden hurdle at Ffos Las. As it happened, a big-field Festival handicap proved too much for Impulsive Star so early in his career, and he was rather bullied out of things as the race was developing, making a bad blunder two out and losing his place in the straight, but his Exeter form was well advertised by the fourth Barney Dwan, who went two places better in the Final. This experience is only likely to aid Impulsive Star's development, while both his background (Irish point winner) and physique very much point to him being a smart long-distance chaser further down the line. Whether or not we see him over fences this season or next, he remains an excellent prospect and is sure to have more to offer. His Exeter win came on soft ground, but it is too early to pigeonhole him as a mud lark, especially given that his other win, a novice at Catterick in January, had come on good going. ***Neil Mulholland***

Conclusion: *Found the Pertemps Final all too much on his final start last season but is better judged on his impressive Exeter win and is sure to have more to offer this season whether remaining over hurdles or going novice chasing*

Just Minded (Ire) h120+
6 b.g Kayf Tara – Georgia On My Mind (Fr) (Belmez (USA))
2016/17 b17.1g* h16s³ h20.5v³ h16.7s* h20.6g² Apr 8

Kayf Tara has stood at Overbury Stud since 2001 but has really started to make his mark at the highest level as a National Hunt stallion over the last couple of seasons, with three Cheltenham Festival winners in 2016 in the form of Thistlecrack, Blaklion and Ballyandy. Last season's long-time Gold Cup favourite Thistlecrack eventually missed the 2017 Festival through injury (though not before landing the King George VI Chase at Kempton) but Kayf Tara still had success in one of the four championship races courtesy of Special Tiara, who won the Queen Mother Champion Chase, while later in the season Tea For Two—who unseated early on in the Gold Cup—landed his second Grade 1 when taking the Bowl at Aintree in April.

Just Minded is one of Kayf Tara's lower-profile prospects at the moment, but just like Thistlecrack, Blaklion and Tea For Two, chasing is likely to be his game, and he looks the type to improve for a switch to fences this season. Just Minded shaped like a stayer when winning a bumper over an extended two miles at Carlisle in November last term, and was suited by the strong pace when getting off the mark over hurdles at Market Rasen in March. He could have been expected to improve when upped to two and a half miles on his final start of last season (lost a shoe on his first try at the trip in January) at Newcastle, but he could only run to a similar level as his win, finishing second to the odds-on favourite Ami Desbois. However, very much a chaser both on looks and on pedigree (dam a winner over fences in France), he remains an exciting novice chasing prospect for this season and should have plenty of good opportunities to win races over fences in the north. **Sue Smith**

Conclusion: *Form over hurdles levelled out last season but looks and pedigree suggest he will improve for the switch to fences, while he also has longer trips still to explore*

Jamie Lynch, Chief Correspondent (Just Minded): *"At Timeform, we try to avoid clichés like Willie Mullins avoids Cheltenham preview nights, but the phrase "anything he does over hurdles is a bonus" was designed for Just Minded. From his build and his breeding to the team around him, everything points to Just Minded taking off for fences, and I fully expect him to graduate to some of the valuable staying handicap chases by the second half of the season."*

Minella Awards (Ire)   h142
6 b.g. Oscar (Ire) – Montys Miss (Ire) (Presenting)
2016/17 h20.5v² h19.8d* h24d* Apr 27]

Hotel Minella is nestled between the Comeragh Mountains and the River Suir in Tipperary and is owned by John Nallen, who explains: "Business is going well. All the horses are named after the hotel in some way, so when people, even in England, hear Minella they always think of the hotel. It's great advertising." Nallen has advertised his own talents with horses, too, selling on the likes of Minella Rocco and Minella Foru in the past, and he recouped £120,000 (much more than his initial €11,000 outlay) when Minella Awards was sold to Highflyer Bloodstock in 2015 after finishing second on his sole point-to-point start. Minella Awards was put into training with Nicky Henderson, where he failed to win in two starts, but he made rapid progress in three subsequent outings for Harry Fry, having switched yards prior to the latest season after being sold as part of the Potensis Bloodstock dispersal.

Minella Awards' new connections showed great patience, with the newly tongue-tied gelding not making his reappearance until January. Two months after finishing second to No Comment on heavy ground at Plumpton, Minella Awards won the EBF 'National Hunt' Novices' Handicap Hurdle Final at Sandown in March, part of a long term plan according to his trainer. Harry Fry explained: "We had campaigned him to qualify for this race. We knew he would be better in the spring." Minella Awards then appreciated the step up to three miles when following up in a twenty-five-runner handicap at Punchestown in April, turning the tables on No Comment with a length success, with the pair five lengths clear of the third. Connections look set to send Minella Awards novice chasing—a BHA mark of 145, 11 lb higher than at Punchestown, would make life tough in handicaps if sticking to hurdles—though it would be no surprise to see him progress into a genuine graded performer over the smaller obstacles if things don't work out over fences. Given his preference for decent ground in the spring, novice races like the JLT and RSA at Cheltenham would be obvious targets, with the handicap chases obvious fall-back options should connections plot another long-term handicap raid. *Harry Fry*

Conclusion: *Rapid progress over hurdles once handicapping for Harry Fry in the spring and has the scope to do well over fences; keep an eye out for a similar campaign this season*

Nic Doggett, Content Manager (Minella Awards): *"Minella Awards failed to win in two starts on soft ground for Nicky Henderson, but he was very well placed for Harry Fry last season, and it's likely that similar awaits over fences this term. Don't expect fireworks over the winter, but, with similarly-shrewd campaigning, Minella Awards could be primed to win a big three-mile handicap chase this spring."*

Minella Suite (Ire)   c100p

6 br.g. Oscar (Ire) – Ballymaguirelass (Ire) (Phardante (Fr))
2016/17 b16d h16.4s⁶ h22.7s⁶ h15.7g⁶ h16d² c15.7s² c21.6sᵘʳ Mar 25

Minella Suite has a long way to go before he becomes an advert for Hotel Minella like Harry Fry's progressive hurdler Minella Awards (highlighted earlier on these pages) and last season's Cheltenham Gold Cup runner-up Minella Rocco (a two-time previous member of our *Fifty*), starting the 2017/18 season as a maiden under Rules, after all, but he remains a work in progress, and there are races to be won with him this term.

A big, lengthy gelding, his spell over hurdles was always going to prove nothing more than a means to an end, and having completed his qualification for handicaps around the turn of the year, Minella Suite caught the eye when finishing second in a conditional jockeys' handicap hurdle at Wetherby in February. Given his build, it was no great surprise that a quick switch to chasing followed and while Minella Suite's future certainly lies over the larger obstacles, a small-field event at Catterick over a trip short of two miles wouldn't appeal as the ideal environment to showcase his ability. He put in an accurate round of jumping, however, and was far from disgraced in chasing home the in-form Sky Full Of Stars. He is well worth another chance to build on the promise of that run, having parted company with Brian Hughes at the second last at Kelso (when holding every chance) next time out, and a BHA mark in the low-hundreds should prove workable when he is faced with longer trips on more galloping tracks this season. *Rose Dobbin*

Conclusion: *Big, lengthy gelding who laid good foundations last season; one to note in handicap chases at trips of 2½m+*

Molly The Dolly (Ire)   b89+

6 b.m. Flemensfirth (USA) – Pistol Flash (Ire) (Pistolet Bleu (Ire))
2016/17 b15.8d³ b16.8v² Mar 5

Molly The Dolly provided the Enniscorthy-based James Doyle (not to be confused with the Flat jockey) with his first career success as a trainer when winning a point-to-point at Cragmore in February 2016, and was subsequently sold for £82,000 to Donald McCain Racing at the Tattersalls Ireland Cheltenham Sale the following month. Despite still having horses with Donald McCain at the time, new owner Dermot Hanafin sent the mare into training with Ian Williams and she shaped with promise in two bumper starts, firstly on her Rules debut at Huntingdon where she showed plenty of ability whilst making the running (eventually finished third), and then at Sedgefield where she was well backed but ran to just a similar level as on debut, keeping on for second under mainly hand-riding.

Dermot Hanafin is not shy about moving his horses between yards to freshen them up, having had recent success on this front with Corrin Wood, who was rejuvenated last season by a switch to Dan Skelton. After the horse finished second at Cheltenham, Hanafin explained: "All we wanted today was for him to finish—he lost the plot but Dan (Skelton) has got him back. He's kept him at the back of the pack and been gentle with him, and no disrespect to Donald (McCain), he needed a change of scenery." The straight-talking Hanafin added: "It was a fantastic ride by Bridget (Andrews), although I had my reservations beforehand, because she rode Debdebdeb for me at Ascot and it didn't go well, but she redeemed herself today." It's clear that Hanafin expects results, and Molly The Dolly has joined Debdebdeb at Skelton's base in Alcester since her latest start. She looks the type to make an impact in mares' novice hurdles this term when granted a true test of stamina (her win between the flags came over three miles on very testing ground). *Dan Skelton*

Conclusion: *Shaped with promise in two bumpers and should relish a stiffer test of stamina over hurdles this season*

Monbeg Aquadude (Ire)   h115
6 b.g Flemensfirth (USA) – Mite Dash (Ire) (Anshan)
2016/17 b16s h19.5s⁵ h19.5v⁴ h20v* h20.9s⁵ Apr 3

Monbeg Dude will probably go down as one of this book's biggest 'nearly' horses of all time after he was scratched from the final *Fifty* in 2012/13 before going on to win a valuable handicap at Cheltenham (at 25/1) and the Welsh National (at 10/1) later that season. We aren't expecting his near-namesake Monbeg Aquadude to reach the same heights over fences this term—he'll only be a novice, after all—but he does look like an interesting chasing prospect for Monbeg Dude's trainer Michael Scudamore.

Bought by Mark Blandford—whose red and black colours are best associated with former Grand Annual winner Next Sensation—for £80,000 as a four-year-old after winning his sole outing in points, Monbeg Aquadude was notably strong in the betting on his Rules debut in a bumper at Ayr in December 2016, but dropped away quickly before the end of the back straight and ultimately shaped as if amiss, eventually trailing home in thirteenth place. The money that had sent him off at 2/1 that day eventually proved significant on his fourth start under Rules, in a maiden hurdle at Ffos Las in March. That end-of-season maiden is unlikely to prove strong form (though the horse he pulled clear with, Warren Greatrex's Savoy Court, cost £70,000 as a three-year-old and had won a bumper), but the BHA handicapper didn't go overboard with Monbeg Aquadude's opening handicap mark (122). Though he disappointed on his handicap debut at Kelso in April he remains one to be positive about and, given his pointing background and physical scope, it would be no surprise were he to make an impact in handicaps over fences next season. ***Michael Scudamore***

Conclusion: *Couldn't justify strong support on bumper debut but did go on to win a maiden over hurdles and looks the sort to take off in handicap chases given his size and pointing background*

Mount Mews (Ire) ★   h140p
6 b.g. Presenting – Kneeland Lass (Ire) (Bob Back (USA))
2016/17 b16.2d* h16.2s* h19.7d² h16.6g* h18.1v* h16.5g² Apr 7

Mount Mews justified his position in last year's *Fifty* in no uncertain terms, winning three of his five races, including the Grade 2 Premier Kelso Novices' Hurdle by forty-nine lengths. He then shaped well on his first try in a Grade 1, leaving the firm impression that he should have finished even closer, when second to Pingshou in the Top Novices' Hurdle at the Aintree festival. He wasn't so positively ridden as the winner in a muddling race and also hinted at inexperience under pressure, perhaps no surprise given that he'd done a lot of his winning on the bridle as he climbed the novice hurdling ranks. Mount Mews had previously shown a lack of concentration when beaten over two and a half miles at Wetherby (matched at 1.01 in-running on the Betfair Exchange), but the feeling is that his future will lie over that distance and further in time—he is bred to be a staying chaser being by Presenting out of a full sister to the high-class Burton Port.

While hopes had been high that Mount Mews could develop into a leading northern hope for either the Neptune or Albert Bartlett Novices' Hurdle at the 2017 Cheltenham Festival, he didn't travel further south than Liverpool over the course of the season, and, kept mainly to flat tracks to date, there appears no reason why connections should try anything different this year. His trainer Malcolm Jefferson has suggested that he will be aimed at the Fighting Fifth Hurdle at Newcastle in early-December, and, given the horse's ability to handle testing conditions, the race looks a good fit. Jefferson knows what it takes to win the race, too, having saddled Dato Star to back-to-back wins in the late '90s. Should Mount Mews not hit the anticipated heights over hurdles then novice chasing, for which he has the build, will beckon. **Malcolm Jefferson**

Conclusion: *Exciting prospect for Grade 1s over the winter months, likely to be kept to flat tracks if his novice season is anything to go by*

Mount Mews (second left) chases home fellow Fifty member Pingshou (right) at Aintree

Mr Big Shot (Ire)   h133p

6 br.g Flemensfirth (USA) – Une Etoile (Ire) (Un Desperado)
2016/17 h16d* h17d* Apr 5

Gene Chandler, who had forty Pop and R&B chart hits between 1961 and 1986, is best known for his 1962 number-one Duke of Earl, however one of his lesser-known songs was Mr Big Shot, which includes the lines:

Hey look at that pretty boy/With no place to go/And that's a Big Shot, yeah yeah/ Money he's got/But friends he has not.

In contrast, it's safe to say that the good-looking equine Mr Big Shot is on the path to bigger and better things judging by his three victories to date, though the way he has steamrollered his opposition so far suggests that he won't have many friends left on the track if continuing in the same vein. He showed useful form when winning at Uttoxeter (by eight lengths) on his only start in bumpers in 2015/16, and quickly bettered that when winning by the same margin on his hurdling debut at Wetherby last January. He had a simple task when following up under a penalty at Carlisle ten weeks later, but impressed with his accurate jumping and how powerfully he travelled before easing clear.

The fact that Mr Big Shot wasn't rushed into action last season, only making his reappearance in January and given a lengthy break before his next start in April, suggests that connections are in no hurry with this big, chasing type. Indeed, Mr Big Shot is bred to be a staying chaser—his dam is a sister to the useful Philson Run, winner of the 2006 Eider Chase at Newcastle—and he looks sure to make his mark in novice chases over further than two miles this season. He remains with bags of potential after just three starts and looks another very exciting prospect for owner Caroline Tisdall. *David Pipe*

Conclusion: *Bred to stay well and could make up into a leading staying novice chaser this season; potential RSA candidate*

No Hassle Hoff (Ire)   h133

5 b.g. Craigsteel – Endless Patience (Ire) (Miner's Lamp)
2016/17 h19.1d^F h25.5s* h24s^3 h24.4d^2 h22.8d^2 h24.7g^4 Apr 8

David Hasselhoff, who made his name in the American TV series Knight Rider, has never been shy of poking fun at himself, including with the 2006 parody Jump In My Car, which reached number three in the UK Singles Chart. No Hassle Hoff had less success with his jumping on his hurdling debut at Fontwell, crashing out at the last when thirty lengths clear, but soon made amends when upped markedly in trip on his next start at Hereford. He then finished a respectable third in the Grade 2 Bristol

Novices' Hurdle at Cheltenham behind Wholestone (strong form), but improved again when narrowly touched off in the River Don at Doncaster at the end of January after a ding-dong battle up the home straight with Constantine Bay, another member of this year's *Fifty* who went on to finish fourth in both the Albert Bartlett and the Sefton at Aintree. No Hassle Hoff had found the Sefton winner The Worlds End too hot to handle in the Prestige at Haydock in February, but with his form looking strong, he was well supported for his next start (his first in a handicap) in a Grade 3 at Aintree on Grand National day. He could finish only fourth but ran well for a young, inexperienced horse, paying for trying to close the gap early in the straight with the winner who had skipped clear a long way from home.

No Hassle Hoff is entitled to progress physically over the summer and while he remains feasibly treated over hurdles, he is a good-topped ex-pointer from a family of staying chasers, and it is over fences where his long-term future lies. It would be no surprise if connections decided to get on with the next stage of his career straight away this season. **Dan Skelton**

Conclusion: *Has the form to figure in handicaps over hurdles from his current mark, but possesses the build and pedigree of a staying chaser and is an exciting novice chasing prospect*

Not Another Muddle   h118
6 b.g Kayf Tara – Spatham Rose (Environment Friend)
2016/17 h20.5v² h19.1v* h17.7v² h16d⁵ Mar 11

In the past, Sandown's Imperial Cup could normally be relied upon to provide some of the strongest two-mile handicap form of the season, but there is no doubt that it has suffered somewhat in terms of quality over the last few years due to its proximity to the Cheltenham Festival. That said, the race continues to produce high-class prospects, with 2016 winner Flying Angel developing into a Grade 1-winning novice chaser last season, while a certain Thistlecrack had finished fifth in the 2015 renewal. London Prize, winner of the race in 2017, has developed into a useful Flat horse over the summer, winning handicaps at Goodwood and Newcastle, but the most interesting jumping prospect from that race could well be Not Another Muddle, who finished fifth.

Not Another Muddle started life with Sheena West, but joined Gary Moore after finishing second in a Fontwell bumper in November 2015. He made his debut for Moore in a maiden hurdle at Plumpton in January 2017, and only went down to an improver who had race fitness on his side. Not Another Muddle went one better thirteen days later in a novice at Fontwell despite pulling hard, but didn't get away with such free-going tendencies on his final two starts of the campaign, including in the Imperial Cup when dropped to two miles. It is still very early days for Not Another

Muddle, however, and he should have gained plenty from his four fairly quick-fire starts over hurdles at the beginning of the year. He will need to settle down in his races but if doing so is probably on a workable handicap mark, while he also looks the type to make a better chaser in time. *Gary Moore*

Conclusion: *Raced too freely when 6/1 for the Imperial Cup on his handicap debut last season but current mark should be well within range if he learns to settle, of interest whether he is kept to hurdles or goes novice chasing*

Overtown Express (Ire)　　　　c144

9 br.g Overbury (Ire) – Black Secret (Gildoran)
2016/17 c17g³ c18.8d⁴ c16.2s* c16.2v⁶ Feb 11

If Big Fella Thanks—who was aged fifteen when third in last season's Foxhunters' at Aintree—is anything to go by, then Overtown Express—a spritely nine-year-old—has a few seasons left ahead of him as a racehorse, especially given that he was nearly eight before he made his debut under Rules. A winning pointer, he was switched to fences after one season over hurdles and made his chasing debut in an interesting Plumpton novice in November, a race featuring the previous season's Champion Hurdle fifth, Top Notch. Overtown Express shaped well in third given the company he was keeping, and had a more realistic assignment in a handicap on his next start at Ascot. Visibility was poor that day, but Overtown Express travelled well through the murk, with (brave) in-running punters matching him at odds as low as 3.2 on the Betfair Exchange. When the field re-emerged before the last fence, Overtown Express had dropped back to fourth, but this still represented a career-best effort for him, and he was found a winning opportunity on his next start in a six-runner handicap chase at Warwick. As an upwardly-mobile novice taking on more exposed sorts, Overtown Express was entitled to win that day, but he did so in such a convincing manner (by seven lengths) that he was worth crediting with further improvement, and connections were probably right to step him up in grade for his next start in the Grade 2 Kingmaker Novices' Chase over the same C&D. Though he was sent off at 5/2 for the Kingmaker, Overtown Express was essentially not up to the much stiffer task, but there will be calmer waters for him to explore this season (has a BHA mark of 141), and he looks sure to win more races, his progression far from over with just four starts over fences under his belt. *Harry Fry*

Conclusion: *Lightly-raced nine-year-old who should have more handicaps in him next season starting out from a BHA mark of 141*

Oxwich Bay (Ire)   h118p

5 b.g Westerner – Rose de Beaufai (Fr) (Solon (Ger))
2016/17 b16.8s* h15.8v³ h15.8d² Jan 25

Oxwich Bay is a half-brother to another member of this year's *Fifty*, Pobbles Bay. The pair are trained by Evan Williams and owned by David Williams, and both are named after areas of coastline on the Gower Peninsula in the county of Glamorgan, South Wales, the area in which Evan Williams' yard is based.

Oxwich Bay is the more lightly-raced of the pair, with just four starts under his belt to date, and given that half-brother Pobbles Bay has shown his best form over trips of three miles and beyond, Oxwich Bay remains with plenty of potential going into the new season with longer trips in mind (yet to tackle further than two miles). After winning a Sedgefield bumper in November (beating Dear Sire, who has since won five times over hurdles), Oxwich Bay was quickly sent hurdling, finishing a good third at Ffos Las behind Robinshill, who had a significant experience edge, having won a handicap off a BHA mark of 127 earlier in the season. Oxwich Bay went one better on his second start over hurdles at Ludlow thirty-five days later, finishing a length and a quarter behind next-time-out winner Brave Eagle, and pulling nine lengths clear of the third Ballymountain Boy, who won a handicap in May from a BHA mark of 115. Oxwich Bay has been handed the same mark after his two placed efforts over hurdles, and this would seem a pretty lenient starting point for him this season, particularly given that he is likely to improve once upped to two and a quarter miles or further. Like his half-brother Pobbles Bay, he is also likely to take well to fences when the time comes, too. *Evan Williams*

Conclusion: *Seems to have been handed a very workable opening handicap mark based on his two hurdles starts last season and will have more to offer this term, particularly when upped in trip*

Pingshou (Ire)   h141

7 b.g Definite Article – Quest of Passion (Fr) (Saumarez)
2016/17 h16.3d⁴ h16.8g* h20.3s⁴ h16.4g h16.5g* h16.5d³ Apr 25

Last season was Colin Tizzard's best ever in terms of both domestic winners (fifty-seven, seven more than his previous highest total) and total earnings (broke the £2 million barrier) but he was unable to add to his total number of Cheltenham Festival winners. That seemed a pretty unlikely scenario nearer the beginning of the season, when Tizzard had three lively Gold Cup candidates in Thistlecrack, Cue Card and Native River, as well as exiting novice hurdler Finian's Oscar. Thistlecrack and Finian's Oscar both missed the Festival through injury, however, while Cue Card and Native River didn't quite cut it in the Gold Cup. There were other disappointments for Tizzard throughout Festival week, too, and the yard went without a winner of any sort from the end of February to the 30th of March.

Things couldn't have been much different for Tizzard at Aintree's Grand National meeting in mid-April, however, with four winners across the week, all in the colours of the yard's new supporters Ann and Alan Potts. Pingshou was one of the four horses who bounced back from a moderate run at Cheltenham to win at Aintree, taking the Top Novices' Hurdle under an excellent, positive ride from Robbie Power. That was a muddling race in which it paid to be prominent, but Pingshou showed his win to be no fluke when showing similar form to finish third in the Herald Champion Novices' Hurdle at Punchestown on his next start. He is very much a chaser on looks (rangy sort) and breeding (full-brother to graded-placed chaser Sizing Platinum), so the fact he managed to reach such heights over hurdles bodes well. His best form came at two miles last season, but he is likely to be effective over further, and will presumably be campaigned over a different trip to Finian's Oscar. **Colin Tizzard**

Conclusion: *Possibly slightly fortunate to have landed a Grade 1 over hurdles last season but promises to be even better over fences given his rangy frame*

Pobbles Bay (Ire) c144

7 b.g Oscar (Ire) – Rose de Beaufai (Fr) (Solon (Ger))
2016/17 c20s* c23.6s* c24s⁵ Jan 14

"A few interesting profiles in this field and it's the sort of race that'll throw up some winners in the coming months" read the header on the Timeform report for Pobbles Bay's chasing debut at Uttoxeter in November, which he won by sixteen lengths. The positive summary of that race was spot on, with three of the finishers in behind Pobbles Bay winning races before Christmas, but even the most optimistic of Timeform reporters couldn't have foreseen just how well the race would work out as the season wore on. Nine horses finished the race, and of the eight that were seen out again, seven went on to win at least once, with fourth Poker School and sixth Brandon Hill each winning their next two starts. Beating that many subsequent winners by a wide margin was always going to spark a fairly defensive response from the BHA handicapper, and Pobbles Bay was 14 lb higher in the weights when he made his second chase start on Welsh National Day at Chepstow the following month. That rise didn't stop him following up by four and a half lengths, however, and he took another step forward with an impressive round of jumping. He was slightly below form on his final start of 2016/17, which came just eighteen days later in a listed race at Warwick, but he can step back into handicaps from a BHA mark of 145 this season, and given that his best performance over hurdles came over three and a three quarter miles at Warwick (second, beaten less than three quarters of a length) he should have more to

Pobbles Bay (left) remains lightly raced over fences

offer when granted an even stiffer test over fences when the mud is flying (raced only on soft/heavy going). **Evan Williams**

Conclusion: *Strong novice handicap form last season and is on the radar for a good staying handicap over trips beyond 3m*

Poetic Rhythm (Ire)   h130

6 ch.g Flemensfirth (USA) – Sommer Sonnet (Ire) (Taipan)
2016/17 b17g⁵ b16g* b16.4s* h16.8g⁵ h20.3s³ h20.3s³ h21.1g Mar 15

Since moving yards to become neighbours with former boss Nigel Twiston-Davies at the beginning of the 2015/16 season, Fergal O'Brien's training operation has gone from strength to strength, and he saddled a record sixty winners in 2016/17, nearly doubling his previous best total amount of prize money, with valuable handicap wins from Chase The Spud and Lord of The Island.

Poetic Rhythm didn't manage to win a race over hurdles from four attempts last term, but he was highly tried after his listed bumper win at Cheltenham in November. He shaped encouragingly in a warm novice behind subsequent Grade 1 winner Pingshou on his hurdling debut, before taking his form up a notch, finishing third in a listed race and then in the Grade 2 Classic Novices' Hurdle at the end of January (both over two and a half miles at Cheltenham). The form of both of those races was well advertised at the Cheltenham Festival later in the season, with the winner of the first, Coo Star Sivola, making the frame in the Martin Pipe, and with Classic Novices' Hurdle winner Wholestone finishing third in the Albert Bartlett. Poetic Rhythm ran in the Neptune at the Festival, but had his slim chance—he was sent off at 66/1—ended when he was badly hampered at the fifth flight. Given what he achieved last season, a novice hurdle race—perhaps at a less competitive track than Cheltenham—will be Poetic Rhythm's for the taking this season, though as a winning pointer we may well see him over fences at some stage. Out of a half-sister to Bog Frog, who won the Grande Course de Haies d'Auteuil (French Champion Hurdle) over an extended three miles, Poetic Rhythm should stay beyond two and a half miles. *Fergal O'Brien*

Conclusion: *Yet to win from four starts over hurdles but was highly tried last season and should win races with sights lowered slightly, while he has longer trips still to explore*

 # Potters Legend   c141p
7 b.g Midnight Legend – Loose Morals (Ire) (Luso)
2016/17 c24g* c20.3s* c24g^2 c22.4d^4 c20.8s^2 c26g^4 c25g^4 Apr 8

Potters Legend must be one of the most consistent jumps horses in training, not finishing out of the frame in all fourteen of his starts across the last two seasons. That in itself is impressive, but he has hardly been wrapped in cotton wool, either, and has contested some of the hottest races in the calendar, including at the last two Aintree Grand National meetings as well as last season's Cheltenham Festival. His fourth in the Kim Muir, where he was beaten just two and a half lengths, is his best effort to date, and he did well to finish so close considering he walked through the nineteenth fence. Jumping errors were a big factor of Potters Legend's first season over fences; he wasn't always fluent when winning his second novices' chase at Bangor in November, and made mistakes when fourth at Newbury in December and second at Cheltenham in January. With that in mind, the application of cheekpieces looked a positive move ahead of his final start of the season in a listed handicap at Aintree, and his jumping was better than it had been on occasions during the season, though his effort flattened out and he was below the form of his Kim Muir fourth, having reportedly lost a shoe. Barring that run, Potters Legend was progressive last season, and looks the type to be around in good staying handicaps for some time to come. He seems sure to win more races this season if brushing up on his jumping slightly. **Lucy Wadham**

Conclusion: *Held his form well last season in some hot races and remains open to further improvement, particularly if cheekpieces continue to aid his jumping*

Sam's Adventure   b109

5 b.g Black Sam Bellamy (Ire) – My Adventure (Ire) (Strong Gale)
2016/17 b16s² b16v* Jan 30

The Peter Easterby-trained mare My Adventure was sent off at just 5/1 for her bumper debut in a twenty-five-runner race at Warwick in January 1994, but ended up finishing a well-held twelfth. She won her next start—a novice hurdle at Sedgefield—but didn't manage to win again after that, though she showed herself to be a strong stayer, finishing second over an extended three miles at Catterick on her penultimate start before she was sold for 2,000 gns at the Doncaster November Sale. Though she lacked a bumper win herself, My Adventure's progeny have had plenty of success in that sphere, with four of her six offspring to run in a bumper having won at least one. The latest in that group is Sam's Adventure, who is three from four in bumpers over the last two seasons. Sam's Adventure was just a couple of months into his fourth year when making his Rules debut at Wetherby in February 2016, and despite being one of the least experienced and, indeed, youngest horses in the field, he handled the extremely testing conditions well, winning by nineteen lengths. With so few getting into that race the form was hard to assess, but Sam's Adventure doubled up a month later in a valuable sales race at Newbury (a race that has featured the likes of Diamond Harry, My Tent Or Yours and Tea For Two in recent renewals), again in very testing conditions. He was kept to bumpers last season and defied a double penalty when beating a subsequent winner at Ayr in January, and with that extra experience under his belt, he will presumably now be sent over obstacles. He looks a highly promising hurdling prospect, particularly when his stamina is drawn out over further than two miles when the mud is flying (raced only on soft/heavy). **Brian Ellison**

Conclusion: *Winner of three of his four starts in bumpers and beaten just a short head in the other, he looks an exciting hurdling recruit, particularly with longer trips in mind; should get some good opportunities this winter*

Sam Spinner   h139p

5 b.g Black Sam Bellamy (Ire) – Dawn Spinner (Arctic Lord)
2016/17 h16.4d* h16.2s² h19.3d* h19.3s* Feb 3

Jedd O'Keeffe's main game is Flat racing, but he often keeps a few horses going over the winter, and thanks to Sam Spinner's four wins from six starts (spanning the last couple of jumps seasons) O'Keeffe's total strike-rate over the last five seasons is actually higher with his jumpers (13%) than it is with his Flat horses (11%).

Sam Spinner's win/run ratio is impressive, and he has only been beaten by two horses during his six-race career. The first of those is Betameche, who got the better of both Sam Spinner and Keeper Hill (who won a listed race over hurdles last season) in a bumper at Wetherby in April 2016 before getting injured, and the second is Mount Mews (another member of this year's *Fifty*) who beat Sam Spinner in a novice at Kelso in December. Sam Spinner was giving a 7 lb penalty away to Mount Mews at Kelso and did well to finish just four lengths behind him at the line, and while Mount Mews is expected to go chasing this season, there's a good chance that the smaller Sam Spinner will stay over hurdles. Despite defying a double penalty in a novice at Catterick in February after beating two subsequent winners with ease at the track in January, he seems to have been handed a workable opening handicap mark by the BHA (136). A really straightforward and likable type, he should make an impact in northern handicaps this season. *Jedd O'Keeffe*

Conclusion: *Took his record to four from six last season when defying a double penalty in a novice at Catterick and should have more to offer from a workable-looking opening handicap mark*

Shivermetimbers   b96+

5 br.g Black Sam Bellamy (Ire) – Kimouna (Fr) (Round Sovereign (Fr))
2016/17 b16v* Mar 12

The mythological pirate's phrase "Shiver me timbers!"—used by the character Long John Silver in Disney's 1950 adaptation of Treasure Island—refers to the breaking (into fragments) of the wooden structures that supported the frames of pirate ships, and one suspects a few timbers may be shivered if the horse Shivermetimbers ever set foot on a wooden ship, given the size of him.

Shivermetimbers is clearly built for jumping obstacles of some sort, so it was very encouraging to see him win his sole start in bumpers last season, especially given he was one of only five first-time-out bumper winners for his yard over the last five seasons. The form of his Warwick win in March is yet to work out, but given his herculean frame he did well to put more than two lengths between himself and a pair of well-bred and fairly expensive types in second and third in a race that developed into something of a sprint finish up the home straight. By Black Sam Bellamy (the sire of The Giant Bolster) and related to several winning jumpers on his dam's side at trips up to twenty-one furlongs, Shivermetimbers is a mouth-watering jumping prospect for the season ahead. **Venetia Williams**

Conclusion: *Rare first-time-out bumper winner for his yard and should take well to jumping obstacles given his size*

Singlefarmpayment $\qquad$ c149

7 b.g Milan – Crevamoy (Ire) (Shardari)
2016/17 c23g³ c23.8d² c25.3g* c20.8sᵇᵈ c25g² Mar 14

Last season's Ultima Handicap Chase had everything a modern-day Festival handicap should contain, right down to a fast-finishing Buywise squeezing into the frame at the last minute. Irish raider Noble Endeavor finished third, with first place fought out between the previous year's winner Un Temps Pour Tout and favourite Singlefarmpayment. Un Temps Pour Tout would be knocking on the door in Grade 1 company with the performance he put up to defy top weight and a BHA mark of 155, the same mark which Gold Cup third Native River had defied when winning the Hennessy and Welsh National earlier in the season. Singlefarmpayment was of course getting plenty of weight from the winner, but his performance was exceptionally polished for a novice in such a competitive environment, and on just his fifth start over fences, looking the winner when he jumped to the front at the last (touched 1.39 in-running on the Betfair Exchange) before narrowly losing out in a prolonged battle up the run-in. There is still a valuable handicap chase to be won with Singlefarmpayment this season from his revised BHA mark of 146, with the BetVictor Gold Cup in November appealing as a potential early-season target given his excellent record at Cheltenham (won both of his other two completed starts at the track), but it would be no surprise to see him play a part in even higher grades further down the line. **Tom George**

Conclusion: *Excellent first season over fences culminated in a narrow defeat to a more experienced type at the Cheltenham Festival and is on the radar to land a similar prize this term*

Snow Leopardess $\qquad$ h137p

5 gr.m Martaline – Queen Soraya (Persian Bold)
2016/17 b16g* h16.3g³ h19.4g* h20.8d³ h20.5g* Mar 25

The BHA have put plenty of focus on boosting the National Hunt race programme for mares over the last few seasons, introducing the Dawn Run Mares' Novices' Hurdle to the Cheltenham Festival in 2015/16, and adding significantly to the races available for mares over fences. A listed mares' steeple chase was introduced at Doncaster in 2014/15, while races of the same ilk were added to the calendar in 2015/16 (Carlisle and Huntingdon) and then again ahead of 2016/17 (Market Rasen, Bangor, Warwick and Leicester).

The latter is particularly good news for connections of Snow Leopardess, who may well end up over fences this season given her build and pedigree (closely related to three-mile chase winner Shah of Persia). Snow Leopardess was sent over to Gowran Park to win a listed bumper at the beginning of last season and perhaps didn't make the strides she was expected to when a beaten favourite on two of her first three starts in novice hurdles, ultimately shaping as though she'd be suited by more strongly-run affairs. That last factor was perhaps the key to her much improved final run of the season in the sixteen-runner Mares 'National Hunt' Novices' Hurdle Finale at Newbury, which she won by four lengths from subsequent winner Copper Kay. A revised BHA mark of 135 probably won't prove beyond her over hurdles if she is granted a similar scenario (also yet to be tried over three miles, which should suit) and with novice chasing also to explore, Snow Leopardess is sure to pay her way this season.
Charlie Longsdon

Conclusion: *Listed bumper winner who ran her best race when taking a valuable mares' handicap hurdle at the end of last season; bred to take to fences and sure to win more races this season*

Thomas Campbell   h138p
5 b.g Yeats (Ire) – Hora (Hernando (Fr))
2016/17 b16.2d* h16.4g* h15.7d* h15.7d⁵ h20.3g⁵ h20g⁴ h19.8g Apr 29

Richard and Lizzie Kelvin Hughes will have been devastated by the loss of their Hadrian's Approach at the latest Cheltenham Festival, the former bet365 Gold Cup winner having been fatally injured when falling in the Kim Muir. There were some positives to be taken from the meeting for the owners, however, with Dusky Legend finishing placed in the Dawn Run Mares' Novices' Hurdle—a race the Kelvin Hughes' sponsor under the banner of their Trull House Stud—for the second year running, while there was also plenty of encouragement to be taken from the performance of Thomas Campbell in the Martin Pipe. Bred at Trull House and now owned in partnership with Mrs Van Geest, Thomas Campbell was a comfortable winner of his first two starts over hurdles at Cheltenham in October and Ascot the following month, but arrived at the Festival on the back of a disappointing effort in the Grade 2 Kennel Gate Novices' Hurdle back at Ascot in December. In hindsight, he probably faced an insufficient test of stamina that day, with the winner dictating a relatively steady pace, and Thomas Campbell duly resumed his progress stepped up to two and a half miles for his handicap debut in the Martin Pipe, closing when not fluent two out, and finishing well to get within four and a quarter lengths of the victor, subsequent Grade 1 winner Champagne Classic. Thomas Campbell was below that form in two subsequent outings at Aintree and Sandown (both at two and a half miles), but shaped on the first occasion as if crying out for a further step up in trip, finishing with plenty left, and leaving the impression three miles will be more than within his range. Still only a five-year-old, he remains open to significant improvement after just six starts over timber, and has the scope to make a chaser. **Nicky Henderson**

Conclusion: *Looks a sure-fire improver for a stiffer stamina test and has the potential to make up into a graded-class novice chaser*

Dan Barber, Jumps Editor (Thomas Campbell): *"It was said that members of the Clarence Club, an exclusive dining society formed by poet Thomas Campbell in the 1820s, had "undue devotion to the grateful grape". Turning to drink might have been a temptation last season for those of us who joined the exclusive punting society centred on the equine Thomas Campbell, whose handicap efforts were characterised by what ifs. Granted more prominent rides and/or a step up in trip this season, it's a good bet that any future imbibing will be borne out of celebration instead of commiseration."*

Topofthegame (Ire)   h138p
5 ch.g Flemensfirth (USA) – Derry Vale (Ire) (Mister Lord (USA))
2016/17 h21.6d* h20.3s⁴ h19.3s² Feb 18

Measuring over seventeen hands and affectionately known as 'The Tank', Denman won the Gold Cup in 2008 and was second in each of the next three renewals, including when beating stablemate Kauto Star to the forecast spot behind Long Run in 2011. Trainer Paul Nicholls has lacked the necessary ammunition to compete in the Cheltenham Festival's crown jewel since that pair's retirement, however, and it looks likely to be a similar story ahead of the 2018 renewal, with Nicholls instead looking further down the line. Indeed, if there is a future Gold Cup winner among the Ditcheat ranks at present, it is more likely to be one of the many exciting novice chasers Nicholls has assembled for 2017/18, including a five-year-old built in seemingly much the same mould as Denman.

"Topofthegame is a huge horse, one of the biggest I've ever trained," explained Nicholls in his Betfair blog last season. "He is going to make a smashing chaser in time." It is hard to disagree with that statement given the promise Topofthegame showed in three starts over hurdles in 2016/17. A winner of his only point in Ireland, he made a successful debut over hurdles at Ascot in December, though he was very nearly undone by inexperience, four lengths clear at the last before running green and ultimately all out to hold on. He built on the promise of that effort when fourth in the Grade 2 Classic Novices' Hurdle at Cheltenham in January, losing momentum after a mistake at the second last, before signing off with a career-best when second back at Ascot in February, holding every chance after jumping the last, and sticking to his task well to be beaten just a neck by Beyond Conceit. A big, raw-boned chasing type on looks, his long-term future certainly looks bright, though it would be no surprise were he to develop into a smart staying novice chaser this season. *Paul Nicholls*

Conclusion: *Tall point winner who is expected to better his useful hurdling form from last season when tackling fences this term; likely to stay 3m*

Uncle Alastair   b98
5 b.g Midnight Legend – Cyd Charisse (Kayf Tara)
2016/17 b16s* b16s* Feb 14

There will be plenty of other bumper winners with sexier profiles than Uncle Alastair going into this season, with neither of his workmanlike wins at Wetherby or Ayr (both of which he won by just a neck) working out that eye-catchingly (though two subsequent winners came out of his first race), but the manner of his victories, where he did plenty off the bridle and showed an excellent attitude, will stand him in good stead for this season, particularly when it comes to stepping up in trip to beyond two miles. Uncle Alastair's pedigree also gives plenty of encouragement that he will improve for more of a stamina test. By Midnight Legend—the sire of last season's Gold Cup winner Sizing John—and out of Cyd Charisse (by Kayf Tara) who stayed three miles, Uncle Alastair is a full-brother to Movie Legend, who was placed over three miles for Lucy Wadham in the most recent season before winning a chase over an extended two miles. Uncle Alastair is one to look forward to when tackling further over hurdles this season and should be well capable of making his mark in northern novices. He has only tackled soft ground to date but both his·dam and full-brother won on good to firm going, so he may well prove to be versatile in that department. *Nicky Richards*

Conclusion: *Looked all about stamina when winning both bumper starts last season; more to come when tackling further over hurdles*

Willie Boy (Ire)   c129p

6 b.g Tikkanen (USA) – Pandora's Moon (Ire) (Tamayaz (Can))
2016/17 h20.1s³ h16.7s³ h20.5d⁵ c20dᶠ c20s* Mar 18

Nothing is certain in sport and racing is no different, just look at Douvan's dramatic defeat in last season's Champion Chase at odds of 9/2-on for one of many examples. There is, however, a certain air of inevitability surrounding fairly expensive point purchases trained by Venetia Williams in the colours of owner Andrew Brooks when those horses eventually tackle fences under Rules. Willie Boy is the latest in a long line of runners to fit that particular profile, and though things didn't quite go to plan when he fell at the first fence on his chasing debut at Sandown in March, having been well backed, normal service was resumed seven days later when he bolted up in a Uttoxeter handicap, travelling strongly and jumping accurately, drawing clear three fences from home and winning by fourteen lengths without coming off the bridle. The handicapper has unsurprisingly taken a fairly dim view of that win and raised Willie Boy 15 lb in the weights, but that was essentially his first chasing start under Rules and he is likely to have even more to offer this season. Given that his original mark had been allotted from three hurdles runs in November and December when he was still showing plenty of signs of inexperience, he at least began life in handicaps from a fairly low base, and he should be winning more races from his new mark of 132.

Venetia Williams

Conclusion: *Made a mockery of opening handicap mark at Uttoxeter on final start and though now up in the weights significantly, looks a typical sort his yard can excel with during the winter months*

Willoughby Court (Ire) ★   h151p

6 br.g Court Cave (Ire) – Willoughby Sue (Ire) (Dabali (Ire))
2016/17 h20.6g² h21s* h21s* h21.1g* Mar 15

Ben Pauling was dealt a huge blow at the beginning of last season when his Grade 1-winning hurdler Barters Hill—a strong and lengthy gelding who looked certain to make a big splash as a novice over fences—suffered a tendon injury on his first start as a chaser and was ruled out for the season. Barters Hill had been a 4/1 chance to give his young trainer a first Cheltenham Festival winner in the 2016 Albert Bartlett but could only manage fourth, but Pauling only had to wait a year to achieve that feat when Willoughby Court edged out Neon Wolf in a thrilling finish to the Neptune.

The ill-fated Neon Wolf may well have justified 2/1 favouritism in the Neptune if not for a peck at the last flight, but Willoughby Court showed gritty determination to hold off his only challenger, having been booted for home two out by rider David Bass,

Willoughby Court (right) fends off the ill-fated Neon Wolf in the Neptune

who had dictated matters from flagfall. Willoughby Court had looked a stayer when winning the Leamington Novices' Hurdle at Warwick over twenty-one furlongs in January, shaping as though a step up to three miles could do plenty for his prospects, and the fact that he is still yet to tackle that distance means that he could still be capable of significant improvement this season. A look at Willoughby Court's pedigree only enforces this view (his dam is a half-sister to Eider Chase winner/Grand National fourth Nil Desperandum), and he looks a smashing prospect for chasing this season, particularly with three miles in mind, while his versatility in regard to underfoot conditions is another positive (won in the mud at Warwick and on good ground at Cheltenham). **Ben Pauling**

Conclusion: *Gritty all-the-way winner of the Neptune last season and yet to tackle 3m which looks as though it will bring out further improvement; an exciting staying chaser in the making*

 Follow us on Twitter @Timeform

Yala Enki (Fr)   c153

7 b.g Nickname (Fr) – Cadiane (Fr) (Cadoudal (Fr))
2016/17 h22.8v³ c22.9s* c24.2s⁴ c26s⁴ c26.2s* Mar 25

Fog caused plenty of problems on British racecourses last winter, including the infamous 'race that never was' at Haydock in December which was won by the Evan Williams-trained hurdler Clyne, though the field were only briefly in view at two points during the whole race (leaving the back straight and again at the third last), and were impossible to make out as they passed the post. No distances were returned and finishing positions had to be taken on trust, so the form was nearly impossible to assess, but ironically the race ended up proving a strong one as the season wore on, Clyne finishing third in the Betfair Hurdle and Le Rocher, Sharp Response and Cooking Fat all winning next time out.

Visibility had been pretty poor for the preceding race on that Haydock card, though the runners in the feature Tommy Whittle Handicap Chase could at least be seen crossing the line, and they were headed by Yala Enki, who'd taken up the running from the fifth fence. After his eight-length win, Yala Enki was turned out just nine days later for the Rowland Meyrick at Wetherby, but understandably found the race coming too

Yala Enki wins the Tommy Whittle Handicap Chase at Haydock

soon and eventually faded into fourth behind the winner Definitly Red. After being given a more substantial break, Yala Enki met Definitly Red again in the Grimthorpe at Doncaster, but despite being sent off 7/2 joint favourite, he was too keen and failed to get home over the furthest trip he'd tackled. Three and a quarter miles proved no obstacle for Yala Enki twenty-one days later at Kelso, however, as he got back to winning ways, crucially settling better in front this time. With only four chasing starts to his name since joining his current stable from France he should have even more to offer this season and can land a couple more valuable prizes in the mud this winter.
Venetia Williams

Conclusion: *Two from four over fences last season and had excuses for both defeats; likely to pick up more races in the north this winter for his shrewd handler*

SECTION

ACAPELLA BOURGEOIS (FR)	48
BACARDYS (FR)	49
CONEY ISLAND (IRE)	50
FAYONAGH (IRE)	50
GREAT FIELD (FR)	51
MICK JAZZ (FR)	52
MONALEE (IRE)	53
MONBEG WORLDWIDE (IRE)	54
OUR DUKE (IRE)	54
PRESENTING PERCY	55

Acapella Bourgeois (Fr)   c152+

7 ch.g Network (Ger) – Jasmine (Fr) (Valanjou (Fr))
2016/17 h24d⁴ c19dᶠ c21.5d³ c19d⁴ c20s* c24s* c24.4g⁶ c24.5d⁵ Apr 25

Few races last season divided opinion as much as the Ten Up Novices' Chase at Navan, which Acapella Bourgeois won by thirty-two lengths, having been completely left alone in front by his rivals and allowed to build up a lead of over twenty lengths before halfway. Unsurprisingly, nothing from the chasing pack could land a blow, including subsequent Brown Advisory & Merriebelle Stable Plate/Ryanair Gold Cup winner Road To Respect (second), and the form was fairly hard to weigh up.

Despite that fact, Acapella Bourgeois was sent off at 5/1 for the RSA Chase on the back of his wide-margin success, but trying to keep tabs on the winner Might Bite on much quicker ground proved too much for him and he dropped away quickly three out. He fared a little better in the Growise Champion Novices' Chase at Punchestown in April, but checked out fairly tamely again, reinforcing the suspicion that he probably needs soft ground to be at his most effective. Acapella Bourgeois' maiden win at Navan took a boost over the summer when the second Arbre de Vie ran two good races at Galway

Acapella Bourgeois slips the field in the Ten Up Novices' Chase at Navan

(finished sixth in the Galway Plate before beating Shaneshill in a minor event at the same meeting four days later), which is perhaps a more solid piece of form than his Ten Up win, and there should be more races to be won with him when he returns to softer ground. With respect to his former handler Sandra Hughes, it would be no surprise to see Acapella Bourgeois improve for the switch to Ireland's eleven-time champion jumps trainer, either. *Willie Mullins*

Conclusion: *Wide-margin novice success last season may not have been all it seemed, but maiden chase form prior to that is solid and is sure to win more races for his new yard when back on softer ground*

Bacardys (Fr) $\qquad$ h150+
6 b.g. Coastal Path – Oasice (Fr) (Robin des Champs (Fr))
2016/17 b16d^3 h16v^F h16d* h18s* h21.1g^{pu} h20g* Apr 28

Patrick Mullins, who rode four winners at the 2017 Punchestown Festival (including Bacardys), was an unlikely hero in his father Willie's ultimately successful challenge for a tenth consecutive Irish trainers' championship—of the yard's nine winners at the meeting, stable jockey Ruby Walsh contributed just two and his main understudy Paul Townend only one.

Patrick Mullins and Bacardys were already well acquainted, having teamed up for two bumper wins the previous season, and they were successfully reunited in the Deloitte Novices' Hurdle in February. Bacardys was subsequently sent off the 4/1 second favourite for the Neptune Novices' Hurdle at Cheltenham, but his race was effectively over when he was badly hampered at the fifth. As a result, he was relatively unfancied for the Tattersalls Ireland Champion Novices' Hurdle on his next start, but he produced a winning performance similar to that of Willoughby Court's in the Neptune on ratings, with Mersey Novices' Hurdle winner Finian's Oscar quickening clear in the straight, before losing momentum at the last and being collared by Bacardys in the final fifty yards. Bacardys won the second of his two starts in points as a four-year-old (fell on debut) and looks sure to stay further than two and a half miles over fences this season. A smart hurdler, he has the potential to be an even better chaser, making races such as the RSA Chase viable long-term targets. *Willie Mullins*

Conclusion: *Looks sure to be suited by 3m+ over fences and, with soft ground not an issue, he should put himself firmly in the Cheltenham Festival frame over the winter months*

Coney Island (Ire)   c159p

6 b.g Flemensfirth (USA) – Millys Gesture (Ire) (Milan)
2016/17 h24d² c20s² c20d* c24d² Dec 29

Our Duke was the first name on the team sheet for our ten Irish prospects in this year's book, but Coney Island ran Jessica Harrington's Irish Grand National winner to just half a length in the Neville Hotels Novices' Chase at Leopardstown in December, and isn't one to forget about as he enters his second season over fences with just three chasing starts under his belt. Coney Island had improved for the step up to three miles as a novice hurdler in 2015/16, winning a valuable handicap at Fairyhouse before finishing second to Bellshill in a Grade 1 at Punchestown, but he was outstayed by Our Duke at Leopardstown, being beaten after touching 1.11 in-running on the Betfair Exchange. While there is no shame in being outstayed by a horse who went on to win an Irish National by fourteen lengths, Coney Island will be fully effective back at two and a half miles given his strong-travelling style, and connections will have plenty of options with him going forward. The form of his Drinmore win over two and a half miles at Fairyhouse initially took a few knocks but looks stronger now, with big spring performances from the second Anibale Fly and fourth Road To Respect, and Coney Island can make up for lost time this season (missed the Cheltenham Festival with a bruised foot, having been short in the betting for both the JLT and RSA). The John Durkan at Punchestown could be an ideal early-season target. *Edward Harty*

Conclusion: *No shame in being outstayed by Our Duke over 3m in Leopardstown Grade 1 last season; not short of speed and worth a go back at 2½m*

Fayonagh (Ire)   b118

6 b.m. Kalanisi (Ire) – Fair Ina (Ire) (Taipan (Ire))
2016/17 b16g b16d* b16v* b16.4g* b16d* Apr 26

Barry Geraghty bought Bobs Worth as a young horse before riding him to win the 2013 Cheltenham Gold Cup, and Jamie Codd will be hopeful that Fayonagh, who he helped buy for her current owners after her Naas win, can reach similar heights. Like the 2015 Champion Bumper winner Moon Racer, Fayonagh started life with a small yard but after being sold for £64,000 at Tattersalls Ireland Cheltenham December Sale, she returned to Ireland to be trained by Gordon Elliott. On her first start for her new stable, Fayonagh gave first notice that she was something out of the ordinary when winning a listed mares' contest at Fairyhouse by twenty lengths, and Codd duly suggested she should run at Cheltenham instead of going for the listed mares' bumper at Sandown the weekend before. The plan looked to have gone awry, though, when Fayonagh remained rooted to the spot for a few seconds when the starter dropped his flag, but, despite still having six ahead of her a furlong out, she burst through late to collar Debuchet in the final strides. Her Punchestown victory was much more straightforward—she made all the running before settling the race in a matter of strides early in the straight. Aries Girl and Refinement, along with the two other mares to have won Punchestown's championship bumper, Liss A Paoraigh and Like-A-Butterfly, all went on to be useful over hurdles at the very least, the last-named winning the Supreme Novices', and there's every reason to think Fayonagh's prospects are just as bright. She is already prominent in the betting for that race (as well as the two mares-only events at Cheltenham) and is reported to have already schooled very slickly over hurdles. **Gordon Elliott**

Conclusion: *Good-looking mare with a fine pedigree (out of a half-sister to very smart hurdler Solerina) who looks set for the very top over hurdles*

Great Field (Fr)　　　　　　　　　　c170p

6 b.g Great Pretender (Ire) – Eaton Lass (Ire) (Definite Article)
2016/17 c16d* c17s* c18s* c16d* Apr 27

Great Field went about his business in quieter fashion than some of the other leading novice chasers last season, but achieved a monster Timeform rating of 170 when landing a four-timer over fences in the Ryanair Novices' Chase at Punchestown in April, meaning only Thistlecrack and Altior were rated higher in last season's novice chase division. Having pulled his chance away when just 7/1 for the County Hurdle in 2015/16 (on his handicap debut and just his second start for Willie Mullins), Great Field was campaigned exclusively in Ireland during 2016/17, making a successful chasing debut at Gowran in late-January and landing a novice at Leopardstown and a listed race at Thurles instead of heading anywhere near Gloucestershire in March. Given the fairly low-key rivals he'd been beating, it was hard to be dogmatic about what Great Field had achieved when winning his first three starts—impressive though he was— but there was plenty more substance added to his Punchestown victory by Ordinary World, who had been placed in the Racing Post Novices' Chase behind Min and in the Arkle behind Altior on his previous two starts. Great Field beat Ordinary World easily, by eleven lengths, and looks well worth his place in top open company this season. His relatively quiet novice campaign may see him go under the radar slightly for the top two-mile contests compared to the other leading second-season chasers Altior and Min. **Willie Mullins**

Conclusion: *Kept a fairly low profile during his first season over fences but confirmed himself as one of the leading novices around when winning a Grade 1 by 11 lengths at Punchestown; more to come*

Great Field is unbeaten in four starts over fences

Mick Jazz (Fr)   h148+

6 b.g. Blue Bresil (Fr) – Mick Maya (Fr) (Siam (USA))
2016/17 h16.5g* h16d² h16d³ h16s* Feb 5

"Remains with plenty of potential; strong traveller and big-field two-mile handicaps may be where he really shines" read the conclusion for Mick Jazz's entry in the 2015-16 edition of this book, and two years and just five starts later, the same sentiment still holds true. That season's campaign, one that had promised so much, was ended almost as soon as it had begun, Mick Jazz giving those who supported him into joint favouritism for the Greatwood Hurdle effectively getting no run for their money as he struggled towards the rear throughout, failing to even complete, and was subsequently found to be suffering from an irregular heartbeat.

By the time Mick Jazz next saw a racecourse almost twelve months later, he had left Harry Fry and crossed the Irish Sea to join Gordon Elliott, and his new handler wasted little time in gaining an overdue first victory, Mick Jazz readily winning a Clonmel novice hurdle. A one and three quarter length defeat to subsequent Supreme winner Labaik in a Grade 3 at Navan the following month reads well, and though Mick Jazz couldn't justify strong market support for a handicap at Fairyhouse on his next start, he got back on the up when fighting off subsequent Grade 1 winner Cilaos Emery in a listed event at Punchestown in early-February. That proved to be Mick Jazz's final start of the season as he was found to be lame on the morning of the County Hurdle at Cheltenham, a race in which he looked to hold a leading chance, but he can be expected to pick up where he left off before the premature conclusion to his 2016/17 campaign. It's hard to believe a valuable two-mile handicap won't fall his way at some stage, and he looks just the sort for a race like the coral.ie Hurdle at Leopardstown in the New Year. **Gordon Elliott**

Conclusion: *Low mileage for a six-year-old and starts the season from a potentially lenient handicap mark; on the radar for a big handicap over 2m*

 # Monalee (Ire) h149
6 b.g Milan – Tempest Belle (Ire) (Glacial Storm (USA))
2016/17 b18s² h22d* h20s² h24v* h24g² h24d⁴ Apr 26

Henry de Bromhead was dealt a big blow at the beginning of the 2016/17 season when it was revealed that leading owners Ann and Alan Potts—responsible for some of de Bromhead's most high profile successes in recent years—were removing their horses from his yard. Those horses included subsequent triple Gold Cup winner Sizing John, amongst others, but de Bromhead ended up having his best season in Ireland in terms of both number of winners and prize money, with his yard one of the main beneficiaries of Gigginstown House Stud's high-profile split with Willie Mullins.

Monalee, owned by Barry Maloney, did his bit for the de Bromhead cause, winning a maiden hurdle at Punchestown in November and a Grade 3 novice at Clonmel in February. Monalee's best effort came in the Albert Bartlett at the Cheltenham Festival, however, finishing second to Penhill having conceded first run. A tall winning pointer, Monalee is the better prospect of the front pair in the Albert Bartlett so far as jumping is concerned, and though he was below his best on his final start of the season at Punchestown, he remains a cracking novice chase prospect for this season and would be a contender for the likes of the RSA Chase, looking just the sort his yard will excel with over fences. **Henry de Bromhead**

Conclusion: *Smart form over hurdles last season, finishing second in the Albert Bartlett; physique and pointing background indicate that he'll be even better over fences*

Monbeg Worldwide (Ire)   **b110**

5 b.g Lucarno (USA) – Molly Duffy (Ire) (Oscar (Ire))
2016/17 b16v* b16v* b16v* Feb 26

Some smart prospects have won what is now the Paddy Power Track My Bet bumper at Naas in late-February in recent years, including the likes of Outlander in 2013 and Killultagh Vic the following year (by sixteen lengths, impressively). Monbeg Worldwide was much more workmanlike in his win in the most recent running of the race, made to pull out all the stops by a rival who had just fair form to his name and winning by just a neck, but he looks a smart stayer in the making, and is likely to have plenty more to offer once tackling trips of beyond two miles this season. The fact that he remains unbeaten in three bumper starts (also one from one in points) bodes particularly well given that he is a big scopey sort who is bred to be effective over much further (dam closely related to Easy Street, who won over an extended three miles for Jonjo O'Neill), and he is one to look forward to when getting a stiffer test of stamina this season. Raced only on heavy ground to date. **Gordon Elliott**

Conclusion: *Unbeaten in bumpers last season from three starts, looking a stayer in the making; will be suited by at least 2½m over hurdles*

Our Duke (Ire)   **c167p**

7 b.g Oscar (Ire) – Good Thyne Jenny (Ire) (Good Thyne (USA))
2016/17 c20d* c24d* c21.3s² c29d* Apr 17

Native River—one of last year's *Fifty*—staked his Cheltenham Gold Cup claim when winning from a BHA mark of 155 in both the Hennessy and the Welsh Grand National, and ended up finishing a creditable third at Cheltenham in March. Our Duke achieved a similar feat at the end of the most recent season when winning the Irish Grand National from a Turf Club mark of 153, and his fourteen-length win marked him down as one of the most—if not *the* most—exciting prospects in National Hunt racing at present. Our Duke began his chasing career with an impressive maiden win at Navan in December, and became a Grade 1 winner just nineteen days later when following up in the Neville Hotels Novices' Chase at Leopardstown over three miles, finding plenty in the closing stages to beat Coney Island by half a length. Our Duke was initially set to be put away after that win with the RSA Chase in mind, but he was seen out earlier than that, running in the Flogas Novices' Chase at Leopardstown in February and relinquishing his unbeaten record over fences, having been unsuited by the emphasis on speed back at an extended two and a half miles. Our Duke's stamina was brought into play significantly more on his next start in the Irish Grand National over three miles and five furlongs, and he relished the test, racing prominently until taking up the running before four out and powering clear of his rivals late on. He looks tailor-

Our Duke looks a prime Gold Cup contender this season

made for the Gold Cup at Cheltenham and only has 3 lb to find on Timeform ratings with last year's winner and stable-companion Sizing John. ***Jessica Harrington***

Conclusion: *Bloodless victory under a big weight in Irish Grand National on just his fourth start over fences marks him down as one of the most exciting prospects in racing this season; looks to have Gold Cup written all over him*

Presenting Percy   h152

6 b.g Sir Percy – Hunca Munca (Ire) (Presenting)
2016/17 b16d h16.5d⁴ h16.2d* h16s* h24d⁵ h24s⁴ h20v* h24g* h24d⁶ Apr 26

"He's on 146 now, 6lb higher than in Ireland, which is not ideal, obviously. It looks like he's going to carry plenty of weight and I'd be very surprised if he was capable of winning a Pertemps off that sort of weight. That will fairly stall him, I think. It can be frustrating [getting different marks] and I don't understand it myself. He's still a novice, he's run in three handicaps but now he has to run with 6lb more here, it's quite confusing."

Davy Russell's comments added fuel to the perceived anti-Irish bias row that was raging before the most recent Cheltenham Festival, with many Irish connections in agreement that there was no need for the BHA to re-assess the marks of Irish runners coming over to race in Britain. In the end, Presenting Percy—the horse Russell had been referring to in his quotes on At The Races in early-March—was one of seven Irish-trained winners of the ten Cheltenham Festival handicaps, and defied his extra 6 lb rise in the Pertemps with plenty to spare. For context, Presenting Percy's performance from a BHA mark of 146 was good enough to have won every previous running of the Albert Bartlett since its inception in 2005, bar Bobs Worth's in 2011, and he was duly sent off at only slightly longer odds than the 2017 winner of that race, Penhill, for the Irish Daily Mirror Novices' Hurdle at Punchestown in April. Presenting Percy didn't run anywhere near his Cheltenham form at Punchestown, but he was probably trained to the minute for the former, and is expected to make his mark at Grade 1 level if kept to hurdles this season. However if quotes from his owner, who describes Presenting Percy as "a horse who could make a lovely chaser" are anything to go by, then it wouldn't be a surprise if he followed the lead of his stablemate Mall Dini—who won the Pertemps in 2016—and went novice chasing this term. Either way, he remains an exciting prospect. *Patrick Kelly*

Conclusion: *Looked a Grade 1 performer in waiting when bolting up in the Pertemps Final; worth another chance at the top level despite flopping at Punchestown*

£10 FREE DOWNLOADS @ TIMEFORM.COM

Join today and we will give you a tenner!

Register a new account with Timeform and we will give you £10 to spend on downloads, tips or subscriptions. No deposit required!

Find out what to spend your free credit on at bit.ly/TFVCode.

Enter voucher code HTF10 when you sign-up.

Flags | Ratings | Insight | Analysis

TIMEFORM

PLAY SMARTER

FIND BETS FASTER AND SMARTER

FILTER

Create a list of horses to bet on today with free **My Timeform Filter**.

Narrow the fields based on criteria you judge to be most important.

Pick the best over course, distance, going, your favourite jockey and more. All at the touch of a button!

At timeform.com and on the App

SECTION

TALKING TO THE TRAINERS 60

Harry Fry 60
Warren Greatrex 60
Nicky Henderson 61
Philip Hobbs 62
Alan King 62
Jonjo O'Neill 63
Ben Pauling 63
David Pipe 64

RISING STARS 65

Rebecca Menzies 65
Olly Murphy 66
Daniel Sansom 67
Mitchell Bastyan 68

ANTE-POST BETTING 69

Betfair Chase 69
Champion Hurdle 71
RSA Chase 72
Champion Chase 72
Cheltenham Gold Cup 73
Grand National 74

LEADING JUMPS SIRES 76

TALKING TO THE TRAINERS

We asked a number of leading National Hunt trainers to pick out a stable star, handicapper, and dark horse to follow for the coming season. Here's what they said ...

Harry Fry

Wins-Runs in Britain/Ireland in 2016/17	**70/293**

Highest-rated horse in training	**Unowhatimeanharry** Timeform Rating h165

Star Performer: Unowhatimeanharry (h165): "He continued his upward curve last season (finishing the season with a career-best win at Punchestown) without quite fulfilling our hopes and dreams of another win at the Cheltenham Festival. He'll follow a very similar pathway to last season, starting with the Long Distance Hurdle at Newbury in late-November."

Handicapper: Melrose Boy (h119): "We thought we'd found a good opening for him at Ludlow in December but ended up bumping into Nicky Henderson's River Wylde, who turned out to be a very decent novice (won the Dovecote and ended up finishing third in the Supreme). He's still a maiden after three goes but we are looking forward to having some fun with him in handicaps from a mark of 123."

Dark Horse: Bullionaire (b105p): "He couldn't have made a more pleasing racecourse debut when winning the Goffs UK Spring Sales Bumper at Newbury in March, and he looks very exciting. We'll probably start off in the listed bumper at Cheltenham's November meeting before deciding whether to stick with bumpers or go over hurdles."

Warren Greatrex

Wins-Runs in Britain/Ireland in 2016/17	**59/332**

Highest-rated horse in training	**Cole Harden** Timeform Rating h155

Star Performer: Missed Approach (c146): "He had a slightly in and out season last year but ran very well to finish second at the Cheltenham Festival in the four miler. He then ran a really good race in the Scottish National, leading to three out, but Cheltenham had probably just left its mark. He's come in looking great and his big objective this season will be the Grand National. He's rated 145, he'll probably have an entry in the Hennessy to start, then we might go to the Welsh National. But he's a horse I like, very straightforward, and I would be quite surprised if he wasn't able to be competitive in these big races."

Handicapper: Groundunderrepair (h112): "He won one last year (maiden hurdle at Lingfield), he's taken a bit of time to come to hand, but he's off a good mark—113—and he's done well over the summer. He's one to keep on the right side of and he should improve a lot this season. He is going to make a chaser, so may switch to fences at some stage."

Dark Horse: Article Fifty: "We bought him at the Doncaster Sales in May (for £115,000), he's by Doyen, and won a two and a half mile point for Phil Rowley. He looks the part here, he's doing everything very nicely. He'll run in a bumper towards the end of October where I'd be surprised if he didn't go close, and then we'll decide whether we stay in bumpers or go hurdling, but he's really exciting."

Nicky Henderson

Wins-Runs in Britain/Ireland in 2016/17	**155/634**
Highest-rated horse in training	**Altior** Timeform Rating c175p

Four-time Champion Trainer Nicky Henderson

Star Performer: Altior (c175p): "I suppose it has to be Altior, although Buveur d'Air isn't far behind. Altior will, I think and hope, start in the Tingle Creek and then take the usual route, all being well, up to the Champion Chase in March. He has summered very well and looks in great order."

Handicapper: Laurium (c141): "Despite his disappointing run at the Scottish Grand National meeting (sent off 9/1 for a three-mile novices' handicap chase in which he was pulled up), I thought he was progressing very well over fences last year and on good ground there could be more to come."

Dark Horse: War Creation (h99): "There wasn't much of her last season but she still managed to win a little novice hurdle (at Ludlow in April). She has summered very well and looks so much stronger that I am hopeful of improvement."

Philip Hobbs

Wins-Runs in Britain/Ireland in 2016/17	**112/604**
Highest-rated horse in training	**Garde la Victoire** Timeform Rating c159

Star Performer: Defi du Seuil (h151p): "He'll probably start off in a four-year-old hurdle race at Cheltenham on the Saturday of the October meeting. We are hoping at this stage that he can make up into a Champion Hurdle contender."

Handicapper: Steely Addition (h106): "He hasn't run for us before, he's had three runs over hurdles elsewhere (for Hugo Froud). He's a five-year-old, he'll go hurdling to start with for us."

Dark Horse: Samburu Shujaa (b95): "He's been placed in a bumper (at Warwick) and he's a horse who ought to improve, he's only a four-year-old. He'll probably go straight over hurdles this season."

Alan King

Wins-Runs in Britain/Ireland in 2016/17	**104/490**
Highest-rated horse in training	**Yanworth** Timeform Rating h164

Star Performer: Yanworth (h164): "The plan is to go chasing, he hasn't schooled yet, but I've always felt that it would not be a problem. I like sending my novices to Exeter, and there are options there in late-October (over two miles two furlongs) or November (over two and a half miles). He obviously proved at Aintree that he gets three miles, but whether he'll go for the RSA or JLT, we'll have to see—I don't think we'll go down the Arkle route!"

Handicapper: Dingo Dollar (h130): "He's a novice (hurdler) that I'm going to send chasing. He's an Irish point winner, he's got a hurdles mark of 130 so he's probably one that we'll go down the novice/novice handicap route with. I just felt everything he did last season over hurdles was a bit of a bonus and I think he could do well."

Dark Horse: Deyrann de Carjac (b77): "We gave him a run in the sales bumper at Newbury, where he was very green but passed a few up the straight. I think he's done very well through the summer, and he's a horse I've always liked. I imagine he'll have another run in a bumper before he goes novice hurdling."

Jonjo O'Neill

Wins-Runs in Britain/Ireland in 2016/17	**78/697**
Highest-rated horse in training	**Minella Rocco** Timeform Rating c167

Star Performer: Minella Rocco (c167): "He was second to Sizing John in last season's Cheltenham Gold Cup (stayed on strongly approaching the last fence) and will be aimed at that race again in 2018."

Handicapper: Call To Order (c118p): "He won over hurdles at Cheltenham off 120 last season (over three miles) and he will go novice handicap chasing this season (shaped encouragingly on chasing debut at Uttoxeter in early-September)."

Dark Horse: Global Citizen: "He won his only point-to-point impressively (at Bellurgan Park by four lengths, before being sold for £275,000 at the Tattersalls Ireland Cheltenham April Sale). He's a nice prospect."

Ben Pauling

Wins-Runs in Britain/Ireland in 2016/17	**32/199**
Highest-rated horse in training	**Willoughby Court** Timeform Rating h151p

Star Performer: Willoughby Court (h151p): "People thought we may have been making a mistake not going three miles last season but he won the Neptune on good ground, it wasn't a slog. We might find ourselves going three miles over fences this season, but we'd like to start off over two and a half at the end of October or early November, and there are races at Huntingdon and Bangor that would be suitable. The Feltham would be where we'd go if we went three miles, and all being well it'll be Cheltenham for either the JLT or RSA."

Handicapper: Bally Gilbert (h112): "He's a horse I've always thought a lot of. He's rated 120, but I always thought he'd be better than that. For one reason or another we haven't had a very clear run with him, but he's returned this season looking fabulous and I'm sure there's plenty of improvement in him. He'll go novice handicap chasing this season."

Dark Horse: Delire d'Estruval (h106): "He's a four-year-old owned by Simon Munir and Isaac Souede who was second in a juvenile chase around Auteuil in the spring, and I think he's quite nice. He may not be the biggest but he's going novice hurdling and I would like to think he's got an exciting campaign ahead of him."

David Pipe

Wins-Runs in Britain/Ireland in 2016/17	**59/489**
Highest-rated horse in training	**Un Temps Pour Tout** Timeform Rating c162

Star Performer: Un Temps Pour Tout (c162): "I put him up last year and he did me proud, winning the Grade 3 Ultima Handicap Chase at the Cheltenham Festival for the second year running, while he was also a good winner on his reappearance over hurdles at Aintree. He has been a great standard bearer for the yard and should be a force in the top staying chases."

Handicapper: Poker Play (h126): "A very nice four-year-old ex-French gelding who finished runner-up on his British debut before running in the Fred Winter at the Cheltenham Festival. He has done well over the summer, strengthening up nicely. He will start off over timber this season, hopefully on a decent handicap mark (131)."

Dark Horse: Warthog (b97): "A good winner of an Irish point-to-point, this five-year-old-son of Martaline showed plenty of promise when a narrow runner-up in a Chepstow bumper and was not disgraced when subsequently running at the Punchestown Festival. A fine, big gelding, he will make a smashing chaser in time, although there are races to be won with him over timber before then."

RISING STARS

Rebecca Menzies

Base	**Morden, County Durham**
First Full Licence	**2013**
First Jumps Winner	**Pistol Basc** Sedgefield 12/11/2013
Total Winners	**41**
Best Horse Trained	**Pain Au Chocolat** Timeform Rating 139

Rebecca Menzies was just eighteen when she joined Ferdy Murphy's yard as a secretary and had worked her way up to assistant trainer by the time Murphy took the decision to sell his yard and relocate to France in 2013. Menzies branched out on her own shortly after that, sending out her first runner in October 2013 from Peter Beaumont's Brandsby yard, but things have really taken off for her since her move to John Wade's yard near Sedgefield racecourse in County Durham at the beginning of the 2016/17 jumps season. Her total number of jumps winners went from seven in 2015/16 to seventeen in 2016/17, and the early stages of this season's jumps campaign have been positive. Like Wade, who still owns horses but who no longer trains, Menzies also mixes both codes of racing, and has enjoyed a good time of things on the Flat during 2017, with over £40,000 in prize money under her belt. She is winning with horses who have been castoffs from some big yards, too. She quickly found the key to four-year-old filly Miss Goldsmith—no mean feat given that she'd raced sixteen times for Richard Fahey without success—on the Flat in 2017, and had previously returned Pain Au Chocolat to winning ways on that horse's first start for her after leaving Dan Skelton. In fact, Pain Au Chocolat's owners Mike and Eileen Newbould have been notable recent supporters of the Menzies yard, also moving Vodka Wells (who won at Hexham in May) to her from Micky Hammond, as well as Royal Mandate and Chateau Chinon, a pair of well-bred and lightly raced ex-Skelton runners who both remain with potential this season. With the support of the Newboulds and Wade, who has moved more of his horses (including the thrice raced Ronn The Conn from Chris Grant) to Menzies from other yards, this season should be even brighter for the operation.

Olly Murphy

Base	**Stratford-Upon-Avon, Warwickshire**
First Full Licence	**2017**
First Jumps Winner	**Gold Class** Market Rasen 09/07/2017
Total Winners	**13**
Best Horse Trained	**Mizen Master** Timeform Rating 120

As the son of Anabel and Aidan Murphy, trainer and bloodstock agent respectively, Olly Murphy has a good pedigree for racehorse training, and was certainly in the right hands during the early stages of his career, having spent over four years as assistant trainer to Gordon Elliott in Ireland. Based just four-hundred metres from where his mother trains in Stratford-Upon-Avon, Murphy has made an excellent start to life in the training ranks, winning with his very first runner (Dove Mountain, on the Flat at Brighton in early-July), and adding another ten winners to his tally during the rest of the month across both codes. Though he is already having plenty of success on the Flat, early signs are that National Hunt horses may take priority for Murphy, with eight of his eleven winners sent out in July having been over jumps. Murphy inherited a number of his mother's horses but has received—and improved—runners from other yards, too. His first jumps winner Gold Class had been unsuccessful in twenty previous starts for Irish trainer Robert Hennessy but produced a career-best to win a lady amateur riders' handicap at Market Rasen on his first start for Murphy following a nine-month break, beating the yard's other runner in the race, Banff, into second. Murphy is only dealing with fairly modest handicappers at present, but more substantial firepower is on the way courtesy of £130,000 ex-Irish pointer Rio Quinto, who was purchased by Murphy's father on behalf of owners Grahame and Diana Whateley. Murphy has already struck up a good relationship with champion jockey Richard Johnson—a regular rider for Elliott's runners in Britain—and even brought leading Irish amateur rider Jamie Codd over to ride at Worcester. Early signs are that he has all the components in place to go right to the very top.

Daniel Sansom

Attached Stable	**Seamus Mullins**
First Ride	**2014**
First Winner	**Kentford Heiress** Fontwell 25/08/2016
Total Winners	**12**
Best Jumps Horse Ridden	**Chesterfield** Timeform Rating 146

After twenty-six years in the saddle riding for a total of around one hundred and seventy-six different trainers and having won two of National Hunt racing's biggest prizes in the Gold Cup and King George VI, Andrew Thornton finally made it into the one-thousand club in December 2016, with a double at Wincanton for trainer Seamus Mullins. Though Thornton didn't officially retire afterwards, he twisted his knee when dismounting his thousandth winner Kentford Myth and has not ridden since. Thornton had been the primary rider for the Mullins yard in recent years and his experience in the saddle would undoubtedly have been missed. Luckily for Mullins, however, he had a very promising conditional jockey waiting in the wings. Daniel Sansom had ridden winners in points and spent five years with Philip Hobbs before joining Mullins, and had his first ride under rules at Fontwell in March 2014. Sansom took a while to get going, needing nearly eighteen months and thirty-three more rides before he got his first winner (Kentford Heiress at Fontwell, taking over from Thornton), but has not looked back since, riding three more winners before landing a big Saturday success aboard Chesterfield in the final race of Aintree's Grand National meeting. Sansom was entitled to claim 10 lb in that race and showed what good value he was, impressing with his judgement, holding Chesterfield up in rear off a brisk pace and slicing through the field to produce his mount to lead at the last. A fifth winner at Plumpton eight days later meant that Sansom was down to a 7 lb claim by the time he got aboard Chesterfield again in the Grade 2 Scottish Champion Hurdle at Ayr, but he demonstrated his skills well again, this time having Chesterfield a little more prominently positioned in a steadily run race and having to get serious with him late on to fight off Zubayr and Sam Twiston-Davies in a tight finish. Sansom has gained plenty of experience riding for Mullins during the summer and was even utilised by Michael Bell aboard Instant Karma in a hurdles race at Stratford in early-May, his first ride for another yard since his career began. There are bound to be plenty of other trainers keen to utilise his claim in the coming months.

Mitchell Bastyan

Attached Stable	**Evan Williams**
First Ride	**2015**
First Winner	**Veauce de Sivola** Lingfield 06/03/2017
Total Winners	**13**
Best Jumps Horse Ridden	**Court Minstrel** Timeform Rating h144

Olly Murphy has hit the ground running in his training career in a remarkable way and similar comparisons can be drawn with what Mitchell Bastyan has done during the infancy of his career as a conditional jockey, landing two winners from his first two rides (including a 50/1 winner) and going on to rack up another four winners in the space of six rides in late June/early July. Bastyan had his first ride under rules (as an amateur) on the Flat in April 2015 for local trainer Simon Hodgson, and also took rides for Brian Barr and Kerry Lee before taking out his conditional licence at Barr's yard in 2017. His first victory came on the Barr-trained Veauce de Sivola at Lingfield and three days later he had doubled his tally with a shock 50/1 winner at Wincanton for Hodgson on General Girling. That horse had failed to complete on its previous two starts but the combination of a change of headgear and Bastyan taking over in the saddle clearly had a positive effect, and he doubled up under a penalty seven days later at Towcester, giving Bastyan winner number three. Hodgson retired from the training ranks in May and winners for Barr dried up as the summer progressed, but Bastyan quickly forged new relations with different trainers to keep the rides flowing, riding his fourth and fifth winners on David Bridgwater-trained runners, and he started life for new boss Evan Williams with a winner on his third ride for the yard. With Williams' long-term retained rider Paul Moloney forced to call time on his riding career at the end of the 2016/17 National Hunt season after failing to recover from a shoulder injury, there are likely to be plenty of opportunities for good rides for Bastyan during the coming season, and he was sent over to Ireland to ride Court Minstrel in the Galway Hurdle in August. Things didn't go to plan on Bastyan's first taste of a top handicap, with Court Minstrel hampered/falling at the very first flight, but this was still a big statement of intent from Williams and further rides in high-profile races are likely to follow as the season progresses.

ANTE-POST BETTING

Timeform's Content Editor Ben Fearnley takes a look at the markets for some of the feature races in the National Hunt calendar and picks out his value bets...

Last year was a tough one for our ante-post picks. Those that showed up in their intended races—which the likes of Ivanovich Gorbatov (Champion Hurdle), Annie Power (World Hurdle), Killultagh Vic (Gold Cup), and both Minella Rocco and Henri Parry Morgan (Grand National) didn't—went off at prices much shorter than they were mentioned at in these pages. That said, Cue Card (5/4 from 9/2) bumped into his superstar stablemate Thistlecrack in the King George and had to settle for second, while God's Own (6/1 from 20/1) would probably have rewarded each-way backers had he jumped a little better in the Champion Chase. As for Grand National hope Vicente (16/1 from 33/1) falling at the first fence at Aintree before going on to show what a good mark he was on by landing the Scottish equivalent for the second successive year... Let's just say it was a season to forget in the ante-post department. The Gold Cup is once again shaping up as one of the races of the coming season, with the returning Thistlecrack joining exciting second-season chasers Our Duke and Might Bite in attempting to de-throne last season's winner Sizing John, who became the first horse to win the Irish Gold Cup, the Cheltenham Gold Cup and the Punchestown Gold Cup in the same season.

Betfair Chase

Sizing John is reportedly going to attempt to land the £1million bonus for winning the Betfair Chase, King George VI and Gold Cup this season, a treble nearly completed by Cue Card in 2015/16. After winning three Grade 1s on the spin at the end of last season and with the speed required for the sharper tests that Haydock and Kempton provide, Sizing John would have a strong chance of going one better than **Cue Card** did when attempting the same treble in 2015/16. The key spring clashes of last season took place without the division's superstar, however, with **Thistlecrack** injured in February and not seen again. Thistlecrack's early season target is reportedly the King George rather than the Betfair Chase, which is reflected in the difference in his price for both Grade 1s (favourite for the King George and 8/1 for the Betfair), leaving Sizing John at the top of the betting. Heading the potential novice challenge is **Might Bite**, last year's dramatic RSA Chase winner, who could make an impact at this level this season given that the standard set by his more experienced rivals (barring Thistlecrack) isn't a high one. He'd be a player if showing up, though he seems to have been campaigned away from testing ground, and with conditions at Haydock in November usually gruelling (four of the last five renewals have been run on heavy ground), he's probably not one to be taking short odds about at this stage. Might Bite was a novice chaser last season but is still two years older than six-year-old **Bristol de Mai**, who was having his second season over fences during 2016/17. With that in mind, we may not have seen the best of Bristol de Mai yet, whose standout performances over fences have both come at Haydock on heavy ground. He won a Grade 2 novice by thirty-two lengths in January 2016, and maintained his unbeaten record at the track when winning the valuable Peter Marsh Chase by twenty-two lengths a year on from that. Given that latter success came from a BHA mark of 153, he was an interesting outsider for last year's Gold Cup, though he promised more than he delivered that day on very different ground. Considering what he achieved last season and his record at Haydock, the Betfair would seem an obvious target for Bristol de Mai, and given his yard, he is perhaps likely to be more forward than some of the other key players, who may well have their eyes on other targets down the line.

Recommendations: Bristol de Mai (10/1)

Bristol de Mai is unbeaten in two starts at Haydock Park

Neptune winner Yorkhill may switch back to hurdles this season

Champion Hurdle

Relying on what connections say can be a dangerous game, especially when it comes to some of Willie Mullins' superstars, who must be placed like pieces of a large jigsaw when it comes to Cheltenham Festival targets. Punters were burnt in a big way during the 2016 Festival when Vautour—whose stated target on the Tuesday of the Festival had been Friday's Gold Cup—was dramatically re-routed to the much weaker Ryanair. We are hoping a similar thing doesn't happen with Yorkhill this season when it comes to the Champion Hurdle, which his connections seem keen on targeting after he lost his unbeaten record over fences with a strange display in the Ryanair Gold Cup Novices' Chase at Fairyhouse, jumping markedly left at his fences and shaping to run out approaching the last. His quirks are an obvious downside, but he has the tools in his armoury to go to the very top of either jumping code, and with signs from his shorter-priced stable companion **Faugheen** not looking overly positive given we didn't see him at all last season, and with **Melon** not able to get the job done in an average Supreme Novices' Hurdle (albeit on only his second start for the yard), Mullins may feel that Yorkhill is his best chance of dethroning **Buveur d'Air**. The current holder isn't a bad favourite, but his four and a half length win over the likable veteran

My Tent Or Yours will probably not have Ireland's champion jumps trainer quaking in his boots. **Defi du Seuil** took everything before him last season and is still unexposed, though his price is about right given how tough it is to graduate from champion juvenile to champion hurdler in just one season.

Recommendations: Yorkhill (12/1)

RSA Chase

Yanworth is reportedly set to go chasing and as a Grade 1-winning staying hurdler last season, he is a fairly short price with most bookmakers for the 2018 RSA Chase. He probably isn't the most straightforward, however, and **Finian's Oscar** and **Willoughby Court** are equally exciting recruits to the chasing ranks. One who is available at slightly bigger odds than that trio makes more appeal from a betting perspective at this stage, however. **Death Duty** was a Grade 1 winner over hurdles last season (won the Lawlor's Hotel Novices' Hurdle by nine lengths) before a disappointing effort in the Albert Bartlett when sent off at just 13/8. Taking a keen grip in a tactical race on the fastest ground he'd encountered was not ideal at Cheltenham (already held when unseating), and despite getting beaten at Punchestown in the Champion Novices' Hurdle (when back at two and a half miles) on his final start of last season, he remains a smashing chasing prospect (well-made point winner). Gordon Elliott and Gigginstown won the Drinmore and the Topaz Novice Chases with No More Heroes in 2015, who went off at 5/2 for that season's RSA, and it is easy to see a similar scenario developing with Death Duty this season, who if anything probably has a bigger reputation than that horse, drawing comparisons with Elliott's Gold Cup winner Don Cossack at a stable tour last season. If the ground came up quick at the Festival, Death Duty would have questions to answer, but he is likely to rack up a sequence in novices over in Ireland before that and will be a much shorter price for this race come March.

Recommendations: Death Duty (20/1)

Champion Chase

At first glance, the Champion Chase looks a tricky race to find value in with last season's Arkle winner **Altior** heading the outstanding **Douvan** at the top of the market. Douvan lost his aura of invincibility—as well as his unbeaten run for Willie Mullins, which stood at thirteen—when reportedly suffering a pelvic fracture in last season's Champion Chase (finishing in seventh), and though many jumps fans will be hoping that he comes back at his best this season, primarily to tackle the outstanding Altior—himself unbeaten in all eleven of his starts over obstacles—this is by no means a guarantee. With Altior short and Douvan risky (along with stablemate **Min**, who raced only twice last season due to a setback) the best bet at this stage could be another Mullins-trained horse, **Great Field**. He went about things in quieter fashion than the top two in the Champion Chase betting last season, starting his campaign in late-January and having only three starts after that, all in Ireland. That didn't stop Great Field achieving a big Timeform rating, however, and he confirmed himself as one of the best novice chasers seen out last season when winning the Ryanair Novices' Chase at Punchestown by eleven lengths with ease. Based on the gap between him and Altior on Timeform ratings (only 5 lb), he looks overpriced at 12/1.

Recommendations: Great Field (12/1)

Cheltenham Gold Cup

The rating **Sizing John** achieved when winning last year's Gold Cup was not an outstanding one (some 12 lb off the rating given to Don Cossack in the previous renewal), and though he went on to land a remarkable hat-trick by adding the Punchestown Gold Cup (bravely fending off both **Coneygree** and **Djakadam**) to the Irish Gold Cup and Cheltenham Gold Cup, he'd still have something to find with an on-song **Thistlecrack**, who produced an outstanding performance to land last season's King George as a novice. Backing horses who ended the previous season with injury problems does come with obvious risks attached, however, which is something that counts against both Thistlecrack and **Douvan**, who has plenty of options this season provided he can overcome the injury he sustained during last season's Champion Chase. The somewhat quirky **Might Bite** is featured prominently in the betting for the Gold Cup, but the feeling is that the King George will be more of a suitable test for him, and with **Native River** and **Minella Rocco** both held by Sizing John in an average renewal last season, it is **Our Duke** who looks the best bet of those at double-figure odds. Our Duke became a Grade 1 winner on just his second start over fences, following up from his Navan maiden win with a determined half-length victory in the Topaz at Leopardstown over three miles, doing well to get back up to win as a series of minor errors took their toll. His jumping was better on his next start (though he did peck at the last) in the Flogas Novices' Chase in February, but he didn't quite have the pace to win back at a shorter trip, having been so strong in the finish over three miles on his previous start. Our Duke had been well fancied for the RSA Chase at the Cheltenham Festival but instead bypassed the meeting in favour of the Irish Grand National at Fairyhouse in April, for which he was sent off a well-backed 9/2 favourite. In the end, the performance he put up to win the Irish National would probably have seen him win the RSA, as he carried 3 lb off top weight to a highly impressive fourteen length victory, though financially his connections had things spot on given he picked up €270,000 for his romp, compared to the £99,662 collected by Might Bite in the RSA. Hopefully the Cheltenham Festival will be on the agenda for Our Duke this season, and he looks one of the most exciting prospects in National Hunt racing at present. With just four chasing starts, there is bound to be more to come, and he is worth getting on-side.

Recommendations: Our Duke (10/1)

Grand National

Those that took the advice in this book to back **Minella Rocco** for last year's Grand National at 33/1 were sitting pretty after his fast-finishing second in the Cheltenham Gold Cup saw his odds for the Aintree showpiece clipped to as short as 8/1. That minor success story didn't last long, however, as he was ruled out of the National a week later, with his older stablemate More of That—sixth in the Gold Cup—the preferred option for Aintree. Not many seven-year-olds run in the National, and that could have been a major factor in determining the decision to miss the race last season, for all that Minella Rocco had appealed as the type to have the tools to deal with the occasion despite his inexperience. The Gold Cup is reportedly on the agenda for Minella Rocco again this season, though his chance of winning that may well be less this time around given that the likes of Thistlecrack and Our Duke are potentially arriving on the scene, and as an eight-year-old with a third season over fences under his belt, he could finally take his chance in a race that has looked tailor-made for him for some time. The definition of insanity is doing the same thing over and over again and expecting different results, but given the potential Minella Rocco possesses for the Grand National, it is hard not to tip him for the race again this season.

Of those that did make it to last year's race it was **One For Arthur** who emerged victorious after putting up a remarkable performance, ridden patiently in a race that didn't favour such tactics but making rapid late headway to eventually win with a bit in hand. He retains a 'p' (meaning he could be capable of better still) on his Timeform rating, which is rare for a horse that has just won the biggest race in the calendar, and he looks to have a good chance of doing a Red Rum by following up in this season's renewal. **Blaklion** went odds-on in-running during last season's race and may well have finished closer to One For Arthur at the line had he not committed for home so early, and the pair generally occupy the top two places in the ante-post betting at this early stage with most bookmakers. **Native River** would be a fascinating National horse, a bold jumper and a strong stayer, but Colin Tizzard has had very few runners in the race, seemingly preferring other options, which tempers enthusiasm somewhat. Gordon Elliott has run plenty in the race since he won the 2007 renewal with Silver Birch, and though a second win has eluded him so far, he went close last year with **Cause of Causes**, who finished second less than a month after winning the Cross Country at the Cheltenham Festival. Tough and likable, Cause of Causes will be popular for the race again this season, but one of Elliott's less exposed runners, **Noble Endeavor**, makes more appeal at a bigger price. Noble Endeavor was let down by his jumping on a couple of occasions during his novice campaign in 2015/16, including when falling when a staying-on sixth in the National Hunt Chase at the Cheltenham Festival, but eventually put it all together to justify some strong support in last season's Paddy Power Chase at Leopardstown in December. The manner of his victory suggested that there could be even more to come from him, particularly back over longer trips (responded to pressure well and won readily) and he improved again to finish third in the Ultima Handicap Chase at Cheltenham, responding to his jockey's urgings whenever he was called upon and being bang in contention going to the last. He was slightly below that form when finishing sixth in the Irish Grand National on his final start of the campaign, but he lost his pitch at a crucial stage (not fluent) before sticking to his task well, suggesting that he is worth persevering with at marathon distances. The Grand National may well be the main aim this season, his third over fences, and he looks worth backing.

Recommendations: Minella Rocco (25/1) and Noble Endeavor (33/1)

LEADING JUMPS SIRES

More than six years have now passed since the death of King's Theatre, but his loss will have been felt more than ever at Ballylinch Stud in a 2016/17 season that saw him crowned the leading jumps sire (by prize money won) for a fifth time. Seasoned campaigners Cue Card and Menorah both contributed with important wins aged eleven and twelve, respectively, Cue Card when adding to his tally at the highest level at Haydock and Ascot, and Menorah when winning the Oaksey Chase at Sandown for the fourth year in succession. Menorah was quickly retired straight after what was the fifteenth win of his lengthy career, however, while Cue Card, although still capable of top-class form last season, is approaching the veteran stage himself. Indeed, with his death in 2011, King's Theatre will likely relinquish his crown in the coming seasons, though it is difficult to pick out his successor with confidence at this stage.

The recently deceased **Presenting** looks best placed to take King's Theatre's title, having finished runner-up to the current champ in each of the last three seasons. JLT winner Yorkhill was Presenting's leading money earner in the latest season, and Willie Mullins' charge remains with the potential to reach the very top in 2017/18, be it over fences or back over hurdles, his connections suggesting after his defeat at Fairyhouse in April that the latter option will come under serious consideration. Interestingly, Ruby Walsh compared him to the 2008 Gold Cup winner Denman—the best progeny of Presenting to have raced over jumps to date—after his Festival victory. Other sons of Presenting to look out for in 2017/18 include *Fifty* member Mount Mews and Movewiththetimes, who ran well for one so inexperienced when second in the Betfair Hurdle at Newbury in February. He has not been seen since, but remains a potentially exciting novice chaser this season.

Beneficial and **Old Vic** are the only other sires among last season's leading bunch to have won the title before. The former, who died in 2013—the same year he was crowned champion—finished fifth in 2016/17, with the smart staying novice chaser A Genie In Abottle and the useful mare Forge Meadow perhaps two of his more interesting prospects for the campaign ahead. Old Vic, who died in 2011, has inevitably featured less prominently in the leading sires' list since his championship winning season of 2007/08, in which Our Vic won Grade 1s at Cheltenham and Aintree, before Comply Or Die's Grand National victory—worth £450,640 alone—sealed the title. Well down the list in 2016/17, Old Vic doesn't have the ammunition to challenge this time round, though it could pay to follow the very smart hurdler Ballyoptic as a staying novice chaser.

Overbury Stud resident **Kayf Tara** was third to King's Theatre and Presenting last season, and could easily have finished much closer but for the injury that brought a premature end to the season for King George winner Thistlecrack. Favourite for the

Gold Cup at the time his problem was diagnosed, the nine-year-old missed out on the opportunity to compete for a first prize of £327,462—earnings that could have put Kayf Tara within £63,000 of King's Theatre. Kayf Tara still enjoyed top level success at the Festival courtesy of Champion Chase winner Special Tiara, though perhaps the most notable feats at the meeting were achieved by his own sire, **Sadler's Wells**. Indeed, the Coolmore legend was the paternal grandsire of six winners at the Festival, including Arkle hero Altior (by **High Chaparral**), Mares' Hurdle winner Apple's Jade (by **Saddler Maker**) and Neptune winner Willoughby Court (by **Court Cave**).

Montjeu, one of the most successful sons of Sadler's Wells on the track and at stud, was also the grandsire of four winners at Cheltenham. Best known over jumps as the sire of Hurricane Fly, Montjeu lacks the firepower to make a title challenge himself—smart hurdler Open Eagle was his biggest earner over jumps in 2016/17—but his influence as a sire of sires in this sphere continues to grow. **Scorpion**, for example, has a top-class chaser to go to war with this season in the form of Might Bite, who won Grade 1s at both the Cheltenham and Aintree festivals. Nicky Henderson's charge has the potential to be a big earner in 2017/18 if his quirky nature—a trait that Scorpion seems to have passed on to some of his offspring—can be kept in check.

Grange Stud, the place of residence for those standing under Coolmore's National Hunt banner, is responsible for **Oscar** and **Milan**, more sons of Sadler's Wells who finished fourth and fifth, respectively, in last season's leading jumps sires list. The former could easily finish higher this time round, with Finian's Oscar, a member of our *Fifty*, and Our Duke, one of the ten prospects nominated in the Irish segment, likely to be competing at the top level. Milan, on the other hand, achieved a better finishing position in the sire list than he otherwise might have done last season, with One For Arthur's National success contributing £561,300 to his overall total. However, Forza Milan, who is a full-brother to the Aintree hero, and Singlefarmpayment have been flagged up as ones to watch in these pages, and should ensure their sire has another profitable campaign.

Flemensfirth is better represented in the *Fifty* than any other stallion, with five of his progeny considered worthy of close attention in 2017/18. Sire of 2010 Gold Cup winner Imperial Commander, it would be no surprise were that race to be a target for Topofthegame in years to come, and he rates a very exciting staying novice chaser in the shorter term, while Coney Island and Waiting Patiently should also have more to offer as second season chasers. Gold Cup winner Sizing John represented **Midnight Legend** with distinction last season and will have a leading chance in all the top staying chases once again, while **Walk In The Park** can be expected to fare better than last term with more luck. The Willie Mullins-trained pair of Douvan and Min both had their seasons curtailed through injury last term, and would have likely taken high rank at the major spring festivals but for their physical issues.

GRAB THE FREE BETS

Find your winners with racing's best ratings and analysis, then 'get on' direct from the Timeform website and App.

For sign-up offers and Timeform exclusives from our partners:

visit timeform.com/freebets

SECTION

TIMEFORM'S VIEW	80
TIMEFORM'S BEST OF 2016/17	107
2016/17 STATISTICS	114

TIMEFORM'S VIEW

Chosen from the Timeform Formbook, here is Timeform's detailed analysis—compiled by our team of race reporters and supplemented by observations from Timeform's handicappers—of a selection of key races from the Cheltenham and Aintree festivals last spring.

CHELTENHAM Tuesday March 14
GOOD

Sky Bet Supreme Novices' Hurdle (Grade 1) (1)

Pos	Btn	Horse	Age	Wgt	Eq	Trainer	Jockey	SP
1		LABAIK (FR)	6	11-7		Gordon Elliott, Ireland	J. W. Kennedy	25/1
2	2¼	MELON	5	11-7		W. P. Mullins, Ireland	R. Walsh	3/1jf
3	8	RIVER WYLDE (IRE)	6	11-7		Nicky Henderson	Nico de Boinville	8/1
4	1¼	BALLYANDY	6	11-7		Nigel Twiston-Davies	Sam Twiston-Davies	3/1jf
5	5	CILAOS EMERY (FR)	5	11-7	(h)	W. P. Mullins, Ireland	D. J. Mullins	12/1
6	hd	BEYOND CONCEIT (IRE)	8	11-7		Nicky Henderson	Noel Fehily	16/1
7	6	ELGIN	5	11-7		Alan King	Wayne Hutchinson	14/1
8	nk	CAPITAL FORCE (IRE)	6	11-7		Henry de Bromhead, Ireland	Davy Russell	50/1
9	3¼	HIGH BRIDGE	6	11-7		Ben Pauling	Mr Alex Ferguson	20/1
10	8	PINGSHOU (IRE)	7	11-7		Colin Tizzard	Aidan Coleman	25/1
11	2½	MAGNA CARTOR	7	11-7		John Joseph Hanlon, Ireland	Rachael Blackmore	200/1
12	nk	BUNK OFF EARLY (IRE)	5	11-7		W. P. Mullins, Ireland	P. Townend	6/1
13	ns	CRACK MOME (FR)	5	11-7		W. P. Mullins, Ireland	D. E. Mullins	11/1
14	56	GLARING	6	11-7		Amanda Perrett	Leighton Aspell	40/1

14 ran Race Time 3m 52.80 Closing Sectional (4f): 55.9s (101.6%) Winning Owner: Mr A. J. O'Ryan

There have been some vintage editions of this race in recent years, with Altior, Douvan and Vautour having won the last 3 runnings, but it will be a surprise if this proves a strong renewal, with several notable absentees—Neon Wolf and Moon Racer aimed elsewhere, Movewiththetimes missing after a set-back—as well as some of the more fancied runners not coming up to scratch; that said, Labaik was a worthy winner on the day, beating the placed horses fair and square, though his tendency not to start makes it difficult to be totally positive about his prospects; the race was run at a muddling gallop, and developed only after 3 out, several not looking at home faced with such a test of speed. **Labaik** can't be trusted but resumed his progress after consenting to set off with the field this time, unbeaten in 3 starts over hurdles when he's got away on terms; held up, travelled well, smooth headway 2 out, led last, kept on well; he's clearly capable of very smart form when he puts his mind to it, though his previous starting misdemeanours will remain a concern until he shows more than once that he's prepared to put his best foot forward. **Melon** had a huge reputation and justified it to a large extent on just his second start in a bona fide race over hurdles, doing well despite keenness off a steady pace, the sort who could well do even better in a more truly-run race; prominent, took keen hold, still going strongly 2 out, every chance approaching last, kept on. **River Wylde** lost his unbeaten record over hurdles, but ran at least as well as previously, just lacking the pace of the first 2; in touch, not settle fully, challenged 2 out, led briefly approaching last, held when mistake last; he may have still more to offer, for a stable whose runners in this race often go on to better things, even after a defeat. **Ballyandy** held leading claims on his win in the Betfair Hurdle, as well as the 2016 Champion Bumper, but he had an unfortunate experience and is better than this; mid-division, not always fluent, baulked second, never looked comfortable after, effort 2 out, stayed on, never landed a blow; he showed himself a smart novice at Newbury and he's the most likely of these to win big races in the future. **Cilaos Emery** ran respectably in a first-time hood upped further in class, lacking a little in know-how and still early days with him; led, shaken up straight, headed before last, weakened. **Beyond Conceit** couldn't improve further faced with this lesser test, looking ideally positioned as the race developed but not picking up at all once ridden; prominent, travelled well, every chance 2 out, ridden after, soon done with; probably needs more emphasis on stamina. **Elgin** was below his previous form, just seeming a bit flat, a slow jump when the race was taking shape not helping; held up, slow 3 out, ridden after, plugged on straight. **Capital Force** had a lot on in this company and did well considering, though he was never involved; in rear, mistake third, labouring 3 out, late headway; he has the physique to make a better chaser, and could be a useful novice next season. **High Bridge**, sixth in the 2016 Champion Bumper, lost his unbeaten record over hurdles, all in all a little disappointing up in grade, even taking into account his rider's being unable to claim; in touch, shaken up 2 out, weakened straight. **Pingshou** hadn't really done enough to justify his place in this field and was already on the back foot when any remaining chance went 2 out; he's a chaser on looks and could well do better over fences next season. **Magna Cartor** was simply out of his depth; always behind. **Bunk Off Early** was well held, but looks worth another chance at this level, a serious mistake coming at a crucial stage; mid-division, yet to be asked for effort when bad mistake 3 out, not recover. **Crack Mome** was the pick of the Mullins quartet on looks, but he failed to run his race, on less testing ground than previously, possibly just not knowing enough at this stage for this sort of test; waited with, not settle fully, effort when slow 2 out, outpaced after. **Glaring** was flying too high in this grade, his jumping again not holding up under pressure; chased leaders, bad mistake second, blundered fifth, left behind after.

Racing Post Arkle Challenge Trophy Novices' Chase (Grade 1) (1)

Pos	Btn	Horse	Age	Wgt	Eq	Trainer	Jockey	SP
1		ALTIOR (IRE)	7	11-4		Nicky Henderson	Nico de Boinville	1/4f
2	6	CLOUDY DREAM (IRE)	7	11-4		Malcolm Jefferson	Brian Hughes	12/1
3	9	ORDINARY WORLD (IRE)	7	11-4		Henry de Bromhead, Ireland	Davy Russell	25/1
4	7	ROYAL CAVIAR (IRE)	9	11-4	(h)	W. P. Mullins, Ireland	R. Walsh	6/1
5	1	FOREST BIHAN (FR)	6	11-4		Brian Ellison	Aidan Coleman	12/1
6	4	SOME PLAN (IRE)	9	11-4	(t)	Henry de Bromhead, Ireland	D. J. Mullins	20/1
7	20	A HARE BREATH (IRE)	9	11-4		Ben Pauling	Richard Johnson	25/1
F		CHARBEL (IRE)	6	11-4	(t)	Kim Bailey	David Bass	9/1
pu		THREE STARS (IRE)	7	11-4		Henry de Bromhead, Ireland	Robbie Power	66/1

9 ran Race Time 3m 54.10 Closing Sectional (3.75f): 51.7s (106.8%) Winning Owner: Mrs Patricia Pugh

A falsely-run renewal, much as the Supreme had been 40 minutes earlier, though that merely masked Altior's superiority rather than proved his undoing, already set to take the measure of pace-setting Charbel when that one's fall 2 out left the door wide open; as such, the bare form—also held down by Ordinary World—looks a little below that achieved in recent years by the likes of Un de Sceaux and Douvan, not to mention the winner's brilliant stablemate Sprinter Sacre, but the case for Altior putting himself firmly in their bracket is no less compelling than it was pre-race. **Altior** could already boast form that would have won him many of the century's Champion Chases and duly cemented his position as the best novice around—and a major threat to Douvan's supremacy in open 2m company—with a more dominant display than the margin might imply, taking his unbeaten run over obstacles to 10; never far away, he jumped boldly save for a peck at the sixth and was closing in on Charbel, set to take over, when that rival's fall left him in front 2 out, the way he opened up on the run-in reminiscent of his rout in last year's Supreme and seeing him put a further 5 lengths between himself and a staying-on Cloudy Dream inside the final 1f alone (only 3 lengths ahead of Ordinary World crossing last), powering past the line; provided all goes well for both in the interim, and neither Altior nor Douvan have even threatened to put a foot wrong to date, the 2018 Champion Chase will be a spectacle to match the very best rivalries in the sport's modern age, with the potential for returning Min to play Well Chief to their Moscow Flyer and Azertyuiop. **Cloudy Dream** was back to looking the high-class novice he'd promised to be early on as he turned the tables on Forest Bihan from Doncaster 7 weeks earlier (preceding second to Buveur d'Air made to look significantly better, too, in the following Champion Hurdle), holding his own in a more demanding environment down South, a superb effort that would have seen him run out a clear-cut winner without a novice as outstanding as Altior in opposition; he arguably did especially well given the way the race went, too, patiently ridden as the pace ahead was stop-start, but Hughes saved every inch of ground on the inside and had him close enough when Charbel's fall saw him left second 2 out, pulling another 8 lengths clear of Ordinary World on the run-in alone but finding an irresistible rival coming home even more strongly; he's bound to win good races in open company, at least whenever Altior isn't on the scene. **Ordinary World** seemed to run well after 11 weeks off, though a good position in a falsely-run race, plus Charbel's fall, were the main factors in his surprising placing, probably not improving much on what he'd been doing in Ireland (behind Min last time); pressed leader, jumped right early, shaken up approaching straight, left in a place 2 out, kept on, brushed aside run-in. **Royal Caviar** faced a stiffer task in this grade, a 9-y-o novice well short of the top bracket over hurdles after all, and it had shown by the end after he'd threatened to be a place threat for some way, a switch to possibly less suitable patient tactics in the face of competition for the lead an unconvincing excuse; off pace out wide early, progress seventh, mistake 3 out, shaken up approaching home turn, no response; he won't be easy to place, certainly once his novice status has expired. **Forest Bihan** might well have caught Cloudy Dream on an off-day at Doncaster 7 weeks earlier but, either way, his jumping was his main undoing, not coping with the stiffer fences half as well as his old rival, left in a hopeless position as a consequence, settled in last from the off and still there when a bad mistake 3 out (had also hit sixth) ended any remaining hopes, plugging on thereafter without making an impression. **Some Plan** wasn't up to this better company, his jumping suffering as well, hitting the third and already beginning to struggle when a worse error 3 out finished him off. **A Hare Breath**, seemingly hard to train, hasn't progressed from his debut in this sphere, though this would have been a bridge too far even if he had; raced off the pace, not fluent eighth, driven after 3 out, made no impression. **Charbel**, not seen since his 6 lengths second to Altior in early-December, would likely to have had to settle for more minor honours behind that brilliant rival had he completed, still in front but finding his advantage narrowing all the while when crumpling on landing 2 out, worth rating somewhere close to Cloudy Dream for all it's hard to be too dogmatic; either way, he's an undeniably smart novice and, though he could easily have got more out of a novice campaign only 3 runs old, he remains with potential with a view to next season and later this, probably starting at Aintree if none the worse. **Three Stars**, who needed to find plenty of improvement at this level after 11 weeks off, broke down after landing awkwardly at the second.

Stan James Champion Hurdle Challenge Trophy (Grade 1) (1)

Pos	Btn	Horse	Age	Wgt	Eq	Trainer	Jockey	SP
1		BUVEUR D'AIR (FR)	6	11-10		Nicky Henderson	Noel Fehily	5/1
2	4½	MY TENT OR YOURS (IRE)	10	11-10	(h)	Nicky Henderson	Aidan Coleman	16/1
3	3	PETIT MOUCHOIR (FR)	6	11-10		Henry de Bromhead, Ireland	B. J. Cooper	6/1
4	3	FOOTPAD (FR)	5	11-10		W. P. Mullins, Ireland	R. Walsh	14/1
5	sh	THE NEW ONE (IRE)	9	11-10		Nigel Twiston-Davies	Sam Twiston-Davies	10/1
6	2¾	SCEAU ROYAL (FR)	5	11-10		Alan King	Daryl Jacob	25/1
10	½	YANWORTH	7	11-10	(s)	Alan King	Mark Walsh	2/1f
7	¾	WICKLOW BRAVE	8	11-10		W. P. Mullins, Ireland	P. Townend	22/1
8	15	BRAIN POWER (IRE)	6	11-10	(s)	Nicky Henderson	D. J. Mullins	13/2
9	14	CYRUS DARIUS	8	11-10		Malcolm Jefferson	Brian Hughes	50/1
pu		MOON RACER (IRE)	8	11-10		David Pipe	Tom Scudamore	10/1

11 ran Race Time 3m 51.00 Closing Sectional (4f): 56.7s (99.4%) Winning Owner: Mr John P. McManus

The absence of the last 2 winners of this race, Annie Power and Faugheen, had led to much talk about this being a substandard Champion Hurdle, and perhaps overall it was, but in Buveur d'Air it had a winner whose performance looks well up to the recent standard for the race and one likely to continue to be a leading player in the division, a certain irony in the fact that both Buveur d'Air and Yanworth had other plans than the Champion Hurdle in the autumn; the race was run at a better pace than the Supreme, leading to a slower finish, though it would be wrong to suggest the first 2, who came from off the pace, were in any way flattered. **Buveur d'Air**, third to Altior in a top-notch Supreme in 2016, might have followed that stable companion to Grade 1 success at this meeting in a novice chase, but instead pitched up here after a mid-season change of plan, his performance well up to standard for the race, the Supreme remaining his only defeat over jumps, while his age poses no obstacle to his returning as a major contender in 2018; held up, tanked along, hit fifth, smooth headway before 2 out, led before last, won readily. **My Tent Or Yours** belatedly showed himself at least as good as when second in this in 2016, now runner-up 3 times in this race as well as in the Supreme as a novice, these his optimum conditions; held up, travelled well, headway 2 out, chased leader last, kept on well, no impression on winner; he's a remarkable horse, with surely the best Festival record of any horse not to win here, just about as good as ever at the age of 10, time a formidable enemy with regard to going one better. **Petit Mouchoir** ran creditably, to a large extent confirming the improvement of his last 2 starts, again attempting to make all but coming up short, needing no excuses; led, mistake 2 out, ridden after, headed before last, faded run-in. **Footpad** ran respectably, never a threat but only a couple of lengths further behind the third than he had been in the Irish Champion; held up, effort 2 out, kept on, never landed a blow; it would be no surprise were he to be campaigned at Auteuil in the spring, while chasing could be an option next season. **The New One** came up short again in a race which just doesn't play to his strengths, his jumping not up to it and lacking the pace required too; close up, not always fluent, outpaced before 2 out; he'd been seriously considered for a run in the Stayers', and it would surely be worth trying him at 3m in the Liverpool Hurdle next month. **Sceau Royal** had a fair bit to find on form and ran about as well as could have been expected upped in grade; held up, shaken up 2 out, made little impression; he's a smart hurdler who could well make an impact if switched to novice chasing next season. **Yanworth** hadn't been convincing, despite winning all 3 of his races this season, and ran below form faced with his stiffest test of the season, taken round the inside (in contrast to the Baring Bingham last season) and almost the first in trouble; in touch, labouring before 2 out; that he's been fitted with cheekpieces on the last 2 starts isn't encouraging and .it may well be that his attitude is starting to fray a little, no surprise given his sire. **Wicklow Brave**, last seen contesting the Melbourne Cup, wasn't disgraced, in form terms at least, on his first start over hurdles since the 2015 Fighting Fifth, though he was rather let down by his attitude at both ends of the race and looks one to treat with some caution; very slowly into stride, in rear, good progress 2 out, shaken up straight, folded tamely. **Brain Power**, kept fresh for this, raced freely and possibly isn't suited by this track, but he left the impression he was amiss more than anything stepping up from handicap company; prominent, close up and still going well 2 out, stopped quickly when shaken up; he'd looked really progressive prior to this. **Cyrus Darius** had looked to retain all his ability in winning in the mud at Kelso, but couldn't confirm that faced with a much tougher test and was well held; raced off the pace, left behind before 3 out. **Moon Racer** was thrown in at the deep end on just his third start over hurdles, running in this in preference to contesting the Supreme, but went as if all wasn't well after 4 months off; prominent, not always fluent, weakened fifth, pulled up 3 out; he would seem to be pretty fragile and will have a bit to prove when next seen.

CHELTENHAM Wednesday March 15
GOOD

Neptune Investment Management Novices' Hurdle (Baring Bingham) (Grade 1) (1)

Pos	Btn	Horse	Age	Wgt	Eq	Trainer	Jockey	SP
1		WILLOUGHBY COURT (IRE)	6	11-7		Ben Pauling	David Bass	14/1
2	hd	NEON WOLF (IRE)	6	11-7		Harry Fry	Noel Fehily	2/1f
3	3¾	MESSIRE DES OBEAUX (FR)	5	11-7		Alan King	Daryl Jacob	8/1
4	4	BURBANK (IRE)	5	11-7		Nicky Henderson	Jeremiah McGrath	50/1
5	1¼	KEMBOY (FR)	5	11-7		W. P. Mullins, Ireland	D. J. Mullins	16/1
6	1½	BRELADE	5	11-7		Gordon Elliott, Ireland	J. W. Kennedy	18/1
7	2¾	KEEPER HILL (IRE)	6	11-7		Warren Greatrex	Gavin Sheehan	25/1
8	½	SKIPTHECUDDLES (IRE)	6	11-7		Graeme McPherson	Kielan Woods	66/1
9	7	DE DOLLAR MAN (IRE)	6	11-7		Evan Williams	Adam Wedge	50/1
10	1	LIVELOVELAUGH (IRE)	7	11-7		W. P. Mullins, Ireland	D. E. Mullins	16/1
11	28	POETIC RHYTHM (IRE)	6	11-7		Fergal O'Brien	Paddy Brennan	66/1
12	2¾	SHATTERED LOVE (IRE)	6	11-0	(t)	Gordon Elliott, Ireland	B. J. Cooper	8/1
F		CONSUL DE THAIX (FR)	5	11-7		Nicky Henderson	Mark Walsh	16/1

pu	BACARDYS (FR)	6	11-7	W. P. Mullins, Ireland	R. Walsh	4/1
pu	BON PAPA (FR)	6	11-7	W. P. Mullins, Ireland	P. Townend	18/1

15 ran Race Time 5m 08.70 Closing Sectional (4f): 56.6s (103.3%) Winning Owner: Paul & Clare Rooney

A better field in terms of physique and probably potential than for the Supreme and a finish fought out by 2 cracking prospects, the winner just edging it after Neon Wolf pecked at the last, the winner having been given the perfect ride, controlling things in front and kicking on after 3 out, catching plenty out behind; the form looks well up to standard for the race. **Willoughby Court**, under less testing conditions, took the step up in grade in his stride, given a ride to make the most of his qualities, his jumping a key asset as well as his gritty determination; dictated, jumped well, went with enthusiasm, kicked on 2 out, challenged late on, found extra; he's a smart young hurdler and clearly an interesting prospect for next season, whether kept to hurdles or sent over fences. **Neon Wolf**, on less testing ground (that a factor in his running here, rather than in the Supreme), lost little in defeat against a really tough and well-ridden opponent, a peck at the last possibly costing him the race; waited with, travelled well, challenged from 2 out, pecked last, rallied well run-in, just failed; he's the most gorgeous looker and if he doesn't make a top novice over fences next season, it will be a major surprise. **Messire des Obeaux** proved better than ever, needing no excuses; waited with, travelled well, challenged 2 out, not quicken straight, kept on; like many of these, he is likely to be going over fences next season and should do well in that sphere. **Burbank** ran easily his best race, doing his best work at the finish upped in trip and sure to progress again as his stamina is further tested; held up, ridden before 3 out, headway entering straight, stayed on; he'd be worth trying in the Sefton over 3m at Aintree and could well be an RSA Chase type for next season. **Kemboy** had very little experience compared to most and did well in this higher grade, the sort to come fully into his own next season; waited with, not settle fully, going well when mistake seventh, ridden 3 out, outpaced next. **Brelade** had been placed in a couple of Grade 1 novices in Ireland but found this stronger company a bit too hot, running to form, the longer trip neither here nor there (likely to suit another day); held up, good progress 3 out, outpaced after next. **Keeper Hill** ran well up in grade, and he might have done even better still without a serious mistake mid-race; held up, blundered sixth, labouring soon after; he is very much a chaser on looks. **Skipthecuddles** was taking a big step up in class and seemed to excel himself, worth giving the benefit of the doubt for the time being, given this was just his third hurdles start; waited with, took keen hold, mistake seventh, labouring soon after; like many of this field, he looks the type to make a chaser next season. **De Dollar Man** needed to improve to figure and wasn't up to the task, running respectably in the circumstances; chased leader, shaken up before 3 out, weakened 2 out; he looks a chaser and could blossom fully over fences next season. **Livelovelaugh**, under less testing conditions, had a bit to find to figure and was soon put in his place when the winner kicked for home; handy, took keen hold, effort 3 out, outpaced next; he's a prospective chaser for next season. **Poetic Rhythm** had plenty on in this company but, in the event, didn't get the chance to show what he could do; in rear, took keen hold, badly hampered fifth, not recover. **Shattered Love** didn't have much to find on best form to figure but looked all at sea away from soft ground; held up, labouring sixth. **Consul de Thaix** fell fatally at the fifth. **Bacardys**, upped in trip, held leading form claims but didn't get the chance to show what he could do, his race effectively over before halfway; held up, badly hampered fifth, not recover, pulled up straight. **Bon Papa** looked a fascinating contender but failed to complete, something evidently not right with him; held up, not settle fully, hampered fifth, effort 3 out, carried head bit awkwardly, no extra, pulled up last, reportedly lost action.

RSA Novices' Chase (Grade 1) (1)

Pos	Btn	Horse	Age	Wgt	Eq	Trainer	Jockey	SP
1		MIGHT BITE (IRE)	8	11-4		Nicky Henderson	Nico de Boinville	7/2f
2	ns	WHISPER (FR)	9	11-4		Nicky Henderson	Davy Russell	9/2
3	10	BELLSHILL (IRE)	7	11-4		W. P. Mullins, Ireland	R. Walsh	5/1
4	8	ALPHA DES OBEAUX (FR)	7	11-4		M. F. Morris, Ireland	B. J. Cooper	6/1
5	30	O O SEVEN (IRE)	7	11-4		Nicky Henderson	Aidan Coleman	14/1
6	13	ACAPELLA BOURGEOIS (FR)	7	11-4		Ms Sandra Hughes, Ireland	Roger Loughran	5/1
ur		MARINERO (IRE)	8	11-4		Henry de Bromhead, Ireland	D. J. Mullins	25/1
pu		BRIERY BELLE	8	10-11		Henry Daly	Tom O'Brien	25/1
pu		OUR KAEMPFER (IRE)	8	11-4	(t)	Charlie Longsdon	Sam Twiston-Davies	20/1
pu		ROYAL VACATION (IRE)	7	11-4	(b+t)	Colin Tizzard	Paddy Brennan	12/1
pu		HERON HEIGHTS (IRE)	8	11-4	(t)	Henry de Bromhead, Ireland	Philip Enright	40/1
pu		AURILLAC (FR)	7	11-4		Rebecca Curtis	Jonathan Moore	100/1

12 ran Race Time 6m 08.60 Closing Sectional (3.75f): 58.0s (97.8%) Winning Owner: The Knot Again Partnership

A remarkable race and a thrilling finish, a trailblazing performance from Might Bite in a Grade 1 having an unexpected twist for the second time this season, on this occasion his quirkiness all but getting the better of him, a son of Scorpion after all, the loose Marinero coming through to give him a lead, after which he ran on well enough to snatch victory; Whisper ran well, his effort on a par with the best winning performances this century, which ranks him alongside Bobs Worth and Denman among others, though a more straightforward Might Bite would have produced an outstanding performance for the race; the pace was strong, which adds to the winner's credit, the start a shambles, the starter seeming to decide there was no chance of aggitated Acapella Bourgeois obeying a standing start and letting the field go when that one was side on, the starters on reviewing the start finding no rider should be reported for contravening the starting procedure—who judges the judges a matter of more relevance. **Might Bite** showed himself to be every bit as good as his performance at Kempton suggested, set to win by perhaps 10 lengths after forcing a strong pace when he all but pulled himself up after the last, only the arrival of a loose horse to give him a lead getting him going again in time to snatch victory on the line; jumped well in main, went with zest, led after first, well clear 3 out, ridden straight, 10 lengths up when mistake last, hung badly right and came almost to a halt, headed final 1f, got going again to regain lead on line; he's a potentially top-drawer chaser, who will be an exciting contender for all the best races next season, but only if his clearly somewhat quirky nature can be contained, his trainer as good as any around for that task. **Whisper**, back at 3m, ran well in a much more searching test of his mettle than the races he'd won here earlier in the season, his jumping showing the strain a little but the way he closed from 3 out highly commendable, albeit set to be a fortunate winner until Might Bite consented to run on in the nick of time; held up, not always fluent, headway 4 out, took second next, kept on well straight, left in front final 1f, caught on line; his age is a bit of a concern for the longer term, but more immediately he could well gain compensation at Aintree, either in the Mildmay or the Manifesto. **Bellshill**, at 3m for the first time over fences, ran as well as could be expected, making his move with the runner-up but just not good enough to go with him in the straight; held up, headway 4 out, not quicken after 3 out; he's still relatively lightly raced over fences and is likely to have a future as a good handicapper at least. **Alpha des Obeaux** was well held, very much on edge beforehand and finding the effort of giving chase to the winner too much from quite a way out, once again reported to have bled, which must be a concern for his future; prominent, not settle fully, labouring 4 out, reportedly bled. **O O Seven** faced a stiffer task in this grade and never looked able to cope with the demands of the race; mid-division, mistake eleventh, never a threat. **Acapella Bourgeois** was well held, fractious beforehand, the effort of trying to keep pace with Might Bite all too much for him in the end; led first, chased leader after, weakened quickly 3 out. **Marinero** was an early casualty, though loose he played a significant role in the finish; prominent, unseated rider third. **Briery Belle** was again below her best against geldings, this her first start over 3m over fences, the trip nothing to do with her poor showing; mid-division, pulled up 3 out, never on terms. **Our Kaempfer** found this a lot tougher than he had handicap company last time; in rear, mistake fourth, driven early final circuit, blundered fourteenth, pulled up before 4 out. **Royal Vacation** wasn't in the same form as last time back in Grade 1 company, oddly not entered in any of the handicaps at the meeting; chased leaders early, settled in touch, ridden before 4 out, no extra, pulled up straight. **Heron Heights** had won here in the autumn but had a lot to find on that form and would surely have made more impact in a handicap; in rear, tailed off 4 out, pulled up. **Aurillac** was found out in better company; raced off the pace, jumped right, hampered sixth, tailed off tenth, pulled up.

Betway Queen Mother Champion Chase (Grade 1) (1)

Pos	Btn	Horse	Age	Wgt	Eq	Trainer	Jockey	SP
1		SPECIAL TIARA	10	11-10		Henry de Bromhead, Ireland	Noel Fehily	11/1
2	hd	FOX NORTON (FR)	7	11-10	(h)	Colin Tizzard	Aidan Coleman	7/1
3	6	SIR VALENTINO (FR)	8	11-10	(t)	Tom George	Paddy Brennan	33/1
4	hd	TOP GAMBLE (IRE)	9	11-10	(t)	Kerry Lee	Davy Russell	20/1
5	1	GOD'S OWN (IRE)	9	11-10		Tom George	A. P. Heskin	6/1
6	nk	TRAFFIC FLUIDE (FR)	7	11-10		Gary Moore	Joshua Moore	50/1
7	4	DOUVAN (FR)	7	11-10		W. P. Mullins, Ireland	R. Walsh	2/9f
8	17	GARDE LA VICTOIRE (FR)	8	11-10		Philip Hobbs	Richard Johnson	14/1
9	13	SIMPLY NED (IRE)	10	11-10		Nicky Richards	Brian Harding	33/1
pu		SIZING GRANITE (IRE)	9	11-10	(t)	Colin Tizzard	Tom O'Brien	50/1

10 ran Race Time 3m 54.20 Closing Sectional (3.75f): 56.6s (97.6%) Winning Owner: Mrs S. Rowley-Williams

At 9/2-on Douvan was the shortest-priced Festival favourite this century, justifiably so given he was 16 lb clear on pre-race ratings and hadn't been extended in 9 previous outings over fences; however, once underway he failed to jump with any fluency and was done for by 3 out, after which it was left for some horses whose limitations are rather better known to fight it out, and while the pair that came clear still put up top-class efforts, it certainly doesn't go down as a vintage Champion Chase, not even the best form shown in a 2m chase in Britain this season, that honour belonging to the Ryanair-bound Un de Sceaux; the winner set a sound pace, racing clear from the fifth until 3 out, and kept just enough in reserve to hold off a runner-up for whom a brief flat spot on the home turn proved costly. **Special Tiara** scotched any suggestion that he's a waning force as he made it fourth time lucky in a race in which he'd finished third in both 2015 and 2016, a performance on a par with the one which saw him chase home Sprinter Sacre and Un de Sceaux last year good enough this time around in a race weakened by Douvan's failure to deliver, and while inevitably much of the post-race analysis will focus on that, Special Tiara was a worthy winner among those that showed their form; disputing the lead from the off, he pressed on before the fifth, continued to jump boldly in a front and held on gamely having jumped the last 2 lengths clear; Sandown and Punchestown are his 2 options for the rest of the season and a reproduction of this will obviously make him a major contender for one or both of those, though there's a fair chance that those races will take a bit more winning than this one did, if the likes of Un de Sceaux, a back-in-form Douvan or even Altior show up. **Fox Norton**, last seen chasing home Altior in the Game Spirit, ran as well as he ever has back at a track where he's built up such a good record, finding the line coming a stride or 2 too early having been tapped for toe slightly after 3 out; in touch, pecked sixth, outpaced 3 out, headway from next, chased leader run-in, stayed on well, just failed; he's never tried 2½m but won't have any problem with the trip judged on this effort and it's no surprise that connections suggested his next race will be the Melling Chase. **Sir Valentino** finished further behind Special Tiara than at Kempton in December but added another high-class effort to his own collection and there can be no doubting the solidity of this run, not quite good enough in the end but doing everything right along the way; held up, travelled well, headway 4 out, went second last, no extra run-in. **Top Gamble** didn't threaten but typically gave his running and nearly snatched third faced with more of a speed test than suits him ideally—it'd definitely be interesting to see him back over 2½m some time soon; mid-division, outpaced 3 out, finished well. **God's Own** looked at the top of his game on his first start for 3 months and would have been third at worst but for serious mistakes at both 4 out and 2 out, doing well to recover from the former (which cost him both momentum and places) but finding the latter (having just made smooth progress into a clear second) finishing him off; he'll presumably have at least one of Aintree and Punchestown on the agenda again and he's clearly every bit as good now as when winning at both last spring. **Traffic Fluide**, back down markedly in trip, proved he retains his ability at the third time of asking this season, never in the hunt but running more or less up to his best, with the way he finished the race off proposing another try at around 2½m; held up, hit 4 out, outpaced next, late headway. **Douvan** lost his aura of invincibility bidding for a third Festival win, faced with more meaningful opposition than for his small-field cakewalks in Ireland earlier this season but more to the point just not on his game, with a totally out-of-character sketchy round of jumping perhaps symptomatic of something troubling him; soon settled behind the leaders, he reached for the third and fourth, got in close to the fifth, was long again at the eighth and was soon on the retreat once asked for an effort after another error 3 out; clearly this defeat doesn't undo everything that's gone before and he still deserves his rating as one of the best jumpers in training, though he'll have a bit to prove next time we see him all the same. **Garde La Victoire** found this much tougher than the handicap he won at Sandown 10 weeks earlier and ran poorly, seen off by the winner in the battle for the lead by the fifth, making a mistake at the next and soon struggling after a worse one

4 out. Simply Ned had a stiff task back from 11 weeks off but even so usually runs better than this; mid-division, not fluent second, weakened soon after 3 out. **Sizing Granite**, last seen finishing mid-field in a Taunton handicap hurdle, had a stiff task but didn't shape with any encouragement; off pace, struggling from seventh, pulled up before 4 out.

Weatherbys Champion Bumper (Standard Open National Hunt Flat) (Grade 1) (1)

Pos	Btn	Horse	Age	Wgt	Eq	Trainer	Jockey	SP
1		FAYONAGH (IRE)	6	10-12		Gordon Elliott, Ireland	Mr J. J. Codd	7/1
2	1¼	DEBUCHET (FR)	4	10-11		Ms Margaret Mullins, Ireland	D. E. Mullins	10/1
3	1½	CLAIMANTAKINFORGAN (FR)	5	11-5		Nicky Henderson	Nico de Boinville	22/1
4	nk	NEXT DESTINATION (IRE)	5	11-5		W. P. Mullins, Ireland	R. Walsh	10/1
5	nk	WESTERN RYDER (IRE)	5	11-5		Warren Greatrex	Gavin Sheehan	7/1
6	5	DANS LE VENT (FR)	4	10-11		Jamie Snowden	Aidan Coleman	100/1
7	1½	AND THE NEW (IRE)	6	11-5		Johnny Farrelly	Brendan Powell	100/1
8	½	MOUNTAIN ROCK (IRE)	5	11-5		A. P. Keatley, Ireland	J. W. Kennedy	66/1
9	½	CAUSE TOUJOURS (FR)	5	11-5		Dan Skelton	Harry Skelton	9/2f
10	¾	NELSON'S TOUCH	4	10-11		Denis Coakley	Nick Scholfield	100/1
11	1½	PERFECT HARMONY (IRE)	5	11-5		Alan King	Ian Popham	33/1
12	1¼	BETTER GETALONG (IRE)	6	11-5		Nicky Richards	Brian Harding	50/1
13	¾	WEST COAST TIME (IRE)	5	11-5	(t)	Joseph Patrick O'Brien, Ireland	Davy Russell	16/1
14	1½	BAKMAJ (FR)	5	11-5		Alan Fleming, Ireland	Denis O'Regan	12/1
15	2¾	CARTER MCKAY	6	11-5		W. P. Mullins, Ireland	Mr P. W. Mullins	11/2
16	3	ROBIN THE RAVEN (IRE)	5	11-5	(s)	Kim Bailey	David Bass	33/1
17	8	QUICK GRABIM (IRE)	5	11-5		R. P. McNamara, Ireland	Noel Fehily	25/1
18	1	IMPERIAL ELOQUENCE (IRE)	5	11-5		Fergal O'Brien	Paddy Brennan	25/1
19	24	MY MATE MARK	4	10-11		Martin Snowden	Tom Cannon	50/1
20	11	IRISH ROE (IRE)	6	10-12		Peter Atkinson	Henry Brooke	12/1
21	43	COPERNICUS (IRE)	5	11-5	(t)	Charlie Longsdon	Richard Johnson	66/1
pu		FISHERMAN FRANK	6	11-5		Michael Blake	Tom Scudamore	66/1

22 ran Race Time 3m 51.20 Closing Sectional (4.0f): 55.7s (101.2%) Winning Owner: Mrs M. Gittins

All bar 2 of the 23 runners had won at least once in what looked an open renewal of the premier bumper of the season, celebrating its silver anniversary, proving a competitive, though perhaps not especially strong, renewal, too many too close up to take a high view, a mare beating a 4-y-o, 2 categories that haven't often figured on the roll of honour, Fayonagh the first one to win since Total Enjoyment beat another in Refinement in 2002, only 2 mares having made the frame since; Fayonagh's performance was, though, one of the more remarkable in the history of the race, the worst sufferer in another messy start, the standard of starting on the day just not good enough, last for much of the way, still only thirteenth early in the straight, but scything through the field in the last 1f, the race well run and the finish dominated by those that had been more patiently ridden—it was also a rather rough race, with plenty looking for room on the approach to the straight, though none obviously unlucky; in addition, the result suggests that Black Op and Daphne du Clos were notable by their absence. **Fayonagh** progressed again, for a stable at the top of its game, producing a remarkable performance, almost undone by the standing start (would surely have been ridden more prominently otherwise) and coming from last place down the hill to sweep to victory; slowly into stride, in rear, still plenty to do 4f out, headway when not clear run and switched approaching straight, still only thirteenth after 2f out, stormed home to lead final 50 yds; she is a particularly taking sort for a mare, with a fine pedigree, and she will surely have a bright future over jumps. **Debuchet** progressed again, just denied by the late surge of the winner, one of the best efforts in this race by one of his age, the fourth 4-y-o to finish runner-up this century, Cue Card the only one to go one better in that time; in touch, travelled well, led over 2f out, kept on well, headed final 50 yds. **Claimantakinforgan** ran his best race yet, his performance suggesting his Doncaster conqueror Black Op would have been a significant player had he taken his chance; mid-division, took keen hold, effort over 3f out, chased leaders home turn, took second 1f out, not quicken; he's clearly a good prospect for novice hurdles next season. **Next Destination** was much improved from debut, looking very much a stayer, lack of experience possibly also a factor; chased leaders early, settled in touch after, outpaced 4f out, rallied home turn, kept on well final 1f, stayed on; likely to make a useful novice hurdler next season. **Western Ryder** ran well, confirming his position as one of the best of the British-trained bumper performers this season, his effort also reflecting well on the absent Daphne du Clos, who would surely have played a major part had she been able to take her chance; held up, shaken up end of back straight, effort when not clear run approaching home turn, kept on well over 1f out, not quicken final 100 yds; bright prospect for novice hurdling next season. **Dans Le Vent** progressed again, more than confirming the form he showed at Newbury, deserving extra credit as he emerged as best of those that raced close to the pace; prominent, led briefly over 3f out, not quicken early in straight, no extra inside final 1f. **And The New**, one of the 2 maidens in the field, showed significant improvement up in grade, faced with much more of a test of stamina, no surprise on pedigree that that would be the case, likely to benefit from further than 2m when he goes over jumps; held up, headway home turn, stayed on. **Mountain Rock**, after 4 months off, ran well upped in grade; held up, travelled well, headway 3f out, shaken up straight, not quicken; he's shown himself a useful performer in bumpers and is likely to have a future as a hurdler. **Cause Toujours**, well backed after 3 months off, failed to progress as expected from his impressive debut, seeming to cope well with the less testing conditions and just not finishing his race; in touch, travelled well, chased leaders straight, weakened final 1f. **Nelson's Touch** ran well upped in grade, the other most inconvenienced by the mess of a start but unable to overcome that as the winner did; slowly into stride, in rear, effort over 3f out, not clear run soon after, plugged on straight; he's done well in bumpers, but he isn't the most substantial and it's possible he'll have more of a future on the Flat than over hurdles. **Perfect Harmony**, on less testing ground, showed something like his debut form, without ever looking a threat, perhaps a bit short on experience for the demands of the race; held up, effort 4f out, made no impression; he was one of the better types and is likely to have a future over jumps. **Better Getalong**, away from the mud, ran about as well as could have been expected upped in grade; held up, headway 3f out, ridden approaching straight, hung left, weakened; he's a likely sort to win a novice or 2 over hurdles in the North next season. **West Coast Time**, on less testing ground, wasn't quite in the same form as previously, shaping as if he'd benefit from even more emphasis on stamina; mid-division, good progress approaching straight, one paced after 2f out. **Bakmaj** was below form, though he met some trouble in a rough race and might well be better judged on previous form; mid-division, travelled well, stumbled approaching home turn, no extra straight. **Carter McKay**, easy to back, looked the pick on form but failed to meet expectations, perhaps closer to the pace than ideal; chased leaders, ridden 4f out, weakened straight; his last win came over 3f further on soft ground and in a small field, all very different circumstances to this. **Robin The Raven** was below form in first-time cheekpieces after 4 months off, possibly not entirely straightforward, though he met trouble as well; prominent, travelled well, ridden and hampered 3f out, left behind soon after, carried head bit awkwardly. **Quick Grabim**, on less testing ground than previously, was again below form, more on in this company obviously but again not finding a lot; held up, not settle fully, had to wait for gap over 3f out, hampered soon after, weakened home turn. **Imperial Eloquence** seemed unlikely to be near good enough and was well held, never figuring; mid-division, labouring over 3f out. **My Mate Mark** was well held, plenty to find up in grade and doing too much in front anyway; led, headed 4f out, weakened quickly. **Irish Roe** was well held after 4 months off, in nothing like the same form as when dead-heating here last time on softer ground; prominent, shaken up 3f out, soon done with. **Copernicus** was well held on his first outing since leaving Mick Halford after 7 months off, pulling too hard for his own good; prominent, not settle fully, ridden over 3f out, weakened soon after. **Fisherman Frank**, after 8 months off, failed to complete; raced off the pace, labouring after halfway, completely tailed off when pulled up straight.

CHELTENHAM Thursday March 16
GOOD

JLT Novices' Chase (Golden Miller) (Grade 1) (1)

Pos	Btn	Horse	Age	Wgt	Eq	Trainer	Jockey	SP
1		YORKHILL (IRE)	7	11-4		W. P. Mullins, Ireland	R. Walsh	6/4f
2	1	TOP NOTCH (FR)	6	11-4		Nicky Henderson	Daryl Jacob	7/2
3	3	DISKO (FR)	6	11-4	(h)	Noel Meade, Ireland	B. J. Cooper	4/1
4	6	POLITOLOGUE (FR)	6	11-4	(h)	Paul Nicholls	Sam Twiston-Davies	10/1
5	9	KILCREA VALE (IRE)	7	11-4		Nicky Henderson	Jeremiah McGrath	22/1
6	19	FLYING ANGEL (IRE)	6	11-4	(t)	Nigel Twiston-Davies	Noel Fehily	9/1
F		BAILY CLOUD (IRE)	7	11-4	(s+t)	M. F. Morris, Ireland	Mark Enright	50/1
F		BALKO DES FLOS (FR)	6	11-4		Henry de Bromhead, Ireland	D. J. Mullins	16/1

8 ran Race Time 4m 59.30 Closing Sectional (3.84f): 55.9s (103.3%) Winning Owner: Andrea & Graham Wylie

Aside from 2015 when Vautour was a brilliant winner, this has tended to fall below the other Cheltenham Grade 1 novice chases, not only with less history and prestige but also a lower standard of winner; this was one of the stronger renewals, however, featuring Top Notch and Disko, who'd both won Grade 1s already, as well as the highly-talented Yorkhill, that trio dominant in the betting, and it looks very solid form; they didn't go a strong pace, but it was fair, and the winner came through smoothly from last place. **Yorkhill** was primed to produce his best performance of the season at this meeting in 2016, when an impressive winner of the Neptune, and took his chase form to a new level as he maintained his unbeaten start over fences back at Grade 1 level, going about it in a familiar manner, saving something back, no doubt that there's more in the tank as and when required; in rear, travelled strongly and jumped fine (helped by keeping to the inside rail given tendency he's shown to jump left), headway when hampered briefly 4 out, in touch next, led soon after 2 out, pecked at the last, idled and driven out; he has the potential to go to the very top in this sphere and will be hard to beat if heading for the Manifesto at Aintree. **Top Notch** has had an excellent novice chase campaign and ran a cracker in defeat in a deeper Grade 1 than he'd won 6 weeks earlier, showing further improvement, and an error 2 out leaves an element of 'what if?', although the suspicion is that Yorkhill would've beaten him anyway, mindful of his idle nature; tracked pace, travelled well, left second 4 out, upsides when bad mistake 2 out, lost momentum, rallied well after last but was held by the winner in the final 50 yds; he's proven himself very tough and reliable. **Disko** has progressed throughout this first season chasing, running even better here a month on from winning the Flogas; prominent, jumped well in main, close up 4 out, went on soon after next, headed after 2 out, one paced run-in; he'll continue to give a good account and might benefit from a return to further (saw race out well on sole try at 3m). **Politologue** ran respectably up in grade, looking more of a match for the principals for a long way, but this stiff track isn't for him and he didn't see things out; in touch, typically travelled well, fourth 3 out, pushed along between last 2 but found less than looked likely; he's shown a real zest and aptitude for chasing and may yet improve his form back at a flatter track. **Kilcrea Vale** was found out in better company, not disgraced, but top-end handicaps are probably where he belongs rather than graded races; close up, led fifth, headed seventh, left in front again 4 out, headed again soon after next, weakened 2 out; a BHA mark of 140 looks fair. **Flying Angel**, who was fitted with a first-time tongue strap, can have this run overlooked; held up, badly hampered eleventh, no chance after. **Baily Cloud** faced a stiff task but crashed out before the race began in earnest; in touch, fell heavily eleventh, too far out to suggest outcome. **Balko des Flos** was in the process of running well when departing, albeit a bit too far out to be suggesting where he'd have finished; went with enthusiasm, led until fifth, led again seventh, yet to be asked for effort when fell heavily 4 out.

Ryanair Chase (Festival Trophy) (Grade 1) (1)

Pos	Btn	Horse	Age	Wgt	Eq	Trainer	Jockey	SP
1		UN DE SCEAUX (FR)	9	11-10		W. P. Mullins, Ireland	R. Walsh	7/4f
2	1½	SUB LIEUTENANT (IRE)	8	11-10	(t)	Henry de Bromhead, Ireland	D. J. Mullins	8/1
3	6	ASO (FR)	7	11-10	(s)	Venetia Williams	Charlie Deutsch	40/1
4	1½	EMPIRE OF DIRT (IRE)	10	11-10	(t)	Gordon Elliott, Ireland	B. J. Cooper	11/4
5	9	JOSSES HILL (IRE)	9	11-10	(s)	Nicky Henderson	Nico de Boinville	9/1
6	9	ALARY (FR)	7	11-10	(t)	Colin Tizzard	Tom O'Brien	33/1
7	2½	UXIZANDRE (FR)	9	11-10	(s)	Alan King	Wayne Hutchinson	6/1
8	2¼	VANITEUX (FR)	8	11-10		Nicky Henderson	Noel Fehily	14/1

8 ran Race Time 5m 09.70 Closing Sectional (3.84f): 56.6s (101.3%) Winning Owner: E. O'Connell

Not only a representative renewal of the Ryanair but a tremendous spectacle, too, on a week already replete with them, Un de Sceaux allowed his head before halfway and able to maintain an advantage that was as narrow at the line as at any stage from a circuit out, the top-class winner doing well to maintain such a gallop but Sub Lieutenant deserving no little credit himself for leaving the chasing pack behind after that group had still been tightly-packed after 3 out. **Un de Sceaux** put up a performance bettered in the history of the Ryanair only by Vautour 12 months earlier and Cue Card in 2013, an idea of the rarified air an on-song Un de Sceaux resides considering that pair's standing, his strong-galloping style proving a more potent weapon over this trip than it had when only third in the Champion Chase last year for all there wasn't much left at the end as Sub Lieutenant reduced the gap from 6 lengths on the run-in; it could have been a different story had

Walsh not allowed him to stride on from the fifth (others might have persisted in trying to restrain him), but Un de Sceaux's exuberance saw him clear by the eighth and, after the advantage had been reduced 3 out, he opened up again at the next, yet to be ridden when another bold leap—his jumping was fault-free following a mistake at the first—at the last removed any real doubt over the outcome; he went to Sandown, the reported end-of-season destination for Altior, following Cheltenham last year, though his yard was in hot pursuit of the British Trainers' Championship at that stage, making a mouthwatering clash more fantasy than realistic, regrettably. **Sub Lieutenant** added another career-best to a season that has been full of them, testament to his new yard, and he might have given Un de Sceaux a real scare had he gone in pursuit sooner under more patient tactics than usual for all that rival did plenty in going clear before halfway, typically jumping well all the same but left behind by the winner early on the final circuit and then meeting trouble after 2 out, closing all the way to the line once in the clear and making up 4 lengths or so on the run-in alone; he's a top-class chaser who'll hopefully be back for another crack next year, clearly good enough to win a more ordinary renewal. **Aso** seemed to excel himself retried in headgear, though he'd already improved around 10 lb this season, giving hope he's full value for another marked step up; in touch early, off pace back straight, ridden after 4 out, effort next, second early in straight, kept on. **Empire of Dirt** had dismissed handicappers over this C&D in the Plate 12 months earlier but found things happening too quickly at this more exalted level this time around, having taken his improvement up another notch at 3m since joining this yard (trainer publicly keen to tackle Gold Cup instead), not jumping/ travelling half as well as he can and unable to get any closer after rallying around the field to threaten briefly approaching 2 out. **Josses Hill** arrived a better model than last year— especially in terms of jumping—only to underperform in this race for the second season in a row, probably of no more than passing interest that both displays have coincided with the fitting of cheekpieces; close up early, lost place gradually back straight, effort again 3 out, no extra between last 2. **Alary** was discussed as a Gold Cup possible on first joining this yard but has yet to show anything on British racecourses to encourage confidence he's near Grade 1 calibre, soon put in his place 3 out this time. **Uxizandre**, refitted with headgear on only his second start since winning this race in 2015, went backwards from his belated reappearance, happy to let the winner get on with it after leading until the fifth but soon going to nothing once things began to take shape in the chasing pack after 3 out. **Vaniteux** has gone sideways rather than forwards this season, and a more demanding race at this trip exposed his stamina deficiencies, making an effort early in the straight but already tiring when blundering 2 out.

Sun Bets Stayers' Hurdle (Grade 1) (1)

Pos	Btn	Horse	Age	Wgt	Eq	Trainer	Jockey	SP
1		NICHOLS CANYON	7	11-10		W. P. Mullins, Ireland	R. Walsh	10/1
2	¾	LIL ROCKERFELLER (USA)	6	11-10	(s)	Neil King	Trevor Whelan	33/1
3	3½	UNOWHATIMEANHARRY	9	11-10	(t)	Harry Fry	Noel Fehily	5/6f
4	3½	COLE HARDEN (IRE)	8	11-10	(s+t)	Warren Greatrex	Gavin Sheehan	9/1
5	12	SNOW FALCON (IRE)	7	11-10		Noel Meade, Ireland	Sean Flanagan	16/1
6	4	CLONDAW WARRIOR (IRE)	10	11-10	(h)	W. P. Mullins, Ireland	Ms K. Walsh	33/1
7	3¾	ZARKANDAR (IRE)	10	11-10	(b+t)	Paul Nicholls	Harry Cobden	25/1
8	3¾	JEZKI (IRE)	9	11-10	(h)	Mrs J. Harrington, Ireland	Robbie Power	15/2

9	2¼	AGRAPART (FR)	6	11-10		Nick Williams	Lizzie Kelly	66/1
pu		SHANESHILL (IRE)	8	11-10		W. P. Mullins, Ireland	P. Townend	16/1
pu		WEST APPROACH	7	11-10		Colin Tizzard	Tom Scudamore	28/1
pu		BALLYOPTIC (IRE)	7	11-10	(t)	Nigel Twiston-Davies	Sam Twiston-Davies	14/1

12 ran Race Time 5m 49.80 Closing Sectional (7.1f): 101.9s (101.7%) Winning Owner: Andrea & Graham Wylie

Having dominated this division in Britain, Unowhatimeanharry set a fairly high standard for this year's Stayers', rated 6 lb ahead of the field coming into the race, but him aside they were a closely-matched bunch and, with him not performing quite to his best, it took less winning than might have been the case; nevertheless, the rating achieved by Nichols Canyon is still up there with recent standards and the form looks reasonably solid with the Long Walk runner-up, Lil Rockerfeller, and previous winner of this race, Cole Harden, part of the quartet that pulled clear; it was a soundly-run race, even tactically, although the winner was given the ideal ride as Walsh sat back and let the other principals battle before making his challenge last of all. **Nichols Canyon** is unexposed as a stayer, this only his second try at 3m, and he relished it, more so than he'd seemed to when sent to the US last May, perhaps just not in peak form that day in hindsight, and though not emphatic he was back to his high-class best to land the most prestigious of his 8 Grade 1s to date under a very well-judged ride, Walsh mindful not to be aggressive with him over this far; held up, travelled fluently, good headway after 2 out, stayed on to lead on the flat, driven out; he's extremely versatile, already a Grade 1 winner at 2m this season after all, but in the Championship races this is likely to remain his trip, away from the testing ground at least, with the division generally a bit weaker, and given he's only 7 there's plenty more mileage in him. **Lil Rockerfeller** has had surprisingly few tries at 3m considering how well he stays and, freshened up by a 10-week break since below form in the Relkeel, he posted a career best, pegged back only by a multiple Grade 1 winner who received an exemplary ride, losing nothing in defeat, and if he'd kept straight at the last and on the run-in he might have held on; never far away, chased leader approaching 3 out, led soon after 2 out, jumped left last, wandered, headed on the flat and then kept on again, giving his all; Aintree may come soon but he's likely to go to Punchestown. **Unowhatimeanharry** had a flawless record over the last 2 seasons, having accounted for most of the field at least once on recent starts, including the runner-up in the Long Walk, but unlike Lil Rockerfeller, who raised his game, he wasn't quite at his best for some reason, looking in the zone for 95% of the race and delivered to challenge by Fehily only to find less than usual, still by no means disgraced; mid-division, travelled well, headway seventh, tracked pace 3 out, chased leader after 2 out, every chance last, edged right, one paced; although a 9-y-o, he doesn't have that many miles on the clock, certainly not over-raced since joining Harry Fry, and he'll still be a force in these top staying races next season, whilst nearer to hand both Aintree and Punchestown give opportunities for compensation. **Cole Harden** wasn't able to repeat his 2015 win in this race, this a stronger renewal, but he ran well, much better than when filling the same spot 12 months ago, confirming his return to form; led, ridden after 3 out, headed soon after 2 out, held when jumped left last, one paced. **Snow Falcon** wasn't disgraced but was beaten further than looked likely most of the way, possibly just finding the race a bit too competitive, with the Irish staying form generally not holding up here; mid-division, mistake 4 out, chased leaders before 2 out, tied up before last. **Clondaw**

Warrior has been competitive all season in the top Irish staying events but this was a bigger ask and found him out; held up, mistakes sixth, seventh, some headway after 2 out, weakened before last. **Zarkandar** had everything right at Haydock last time, with a small field and flat track, and this underlines that he's not up to it at this level nowadays; held up, took closer order seventh, untidy 3 out, effort 2 out, weakened before last. **Jezki** didn't get home faced with a more severe test at this trip than when beating Hurricane Fly (himself not a stayer) at Punchestown in 2015, shaping better than the distance beaten suggests; in rear, travelled well, headway 2 out, in touch home turn but found little, the emphasis on stamina all too much for him. **Agrapart** found this too competitive and is possibly a bit flattered by his rating from the Relkeel (standout effort) in rear, jumped none too fluently, outpaced 3 out, made no impression. **Shaneshill** had been runner-up at this meeting for each of the past 3 years but failed to give his running this time around, clearly not 100% on the day; mid-division, weakened after 2 out, pulled up before last, possibly amiss. **West Approach** shaped as if amiss; chased leaders, flattened 2 out, dropped away quickly and was pulled up before the last, something not right. **Ballyoptic**, in first-time tongue strap, clearly wasn't 100% on the day; chased leaders, made mistakes, ridden between 3 out and 2 out, weakened, behind when pulled up before last.

CHELTENHAM Friday March 17
GOOD

JCB Triumph Hurdle (Grade 1) (1)

Pos	Btn	Horse	Age	Wgt	Eq	Trainer	Jockey	SP
1		DEFI DU SEUIL (FR)	4	11-0		Philip Hobbs	Richard Johnson	5/2f
2	5	MEGA FORTUNE (FR)	4	11-0	(s)	Gordon Elliott, Ireland	Davy Russell	7/1
3	sh	BAPAUME (FR)	4	11-0		W. P. Mullins, Ireland	R. Walsh	10/1
4	2	EX PATRIOT (IRE)	4	11-0		Ellmarie Holden, Ireland	Rachael Blackmore	28/1
5	½	LANDOFHOPEANDGLORY (IRE)	4	11-0	(t)	Joseph Patrick O'Brien, Ireland	Robbie Power	8/1
6	2½	CHARLI PARCS (FR)	4	11-0		Nicky Henderson	Noel Fehily	9/2
7	¾	COEUR DE LION	4	11-0		Alan King	Tom Cannon	33/1
8	3¼	LANDIN (GER)	4	11-0		Seamus Mullins	Jeremiah McGrath	150/1
9	½	MAGIE DU MA (FR)	4	10-7	(h)	David Pipe	Tom Scudamore	40/1
10	5	MASTER BLUEYES (IRE)	4	11-0		Alan King	Wayne Hutchinson	8/1
11	1¾	DINARIA DES OBEAUX (FR)	4	10-7		Gordon Elliott, Ireland	B. J. Cooper	10/1
12	1	EVENING HUSH (IRE)	4	10-7		Evan Williams	Adam Wedge	50/1
13	11	DANDY MAG (FR)	4	11-0		W. P. Mullins, Ireland	P. Townend	22/1
14	16	I SEE YOU WELL (FR)	4	11-0		Seamus Mullins	Jamie Moore	200/1
15	1	SOLDIER IN ACTION (FR)	4	11-0		Nicky Henderson	Nico de Boinville	16/1

15 ran   Race Time 4m 00.00 Closing Sectional (7.1f): 101.3s (100.1%) Winning Owner: Mr John P. McManus

A well-contested edition of the top juvenile hurdle of the season, but it was run at no more than a fair pace, taking shape only from 2 out, and it's hard to rate the race as even an average renewal in form terms, though the winner is likely to have been even more clear-cut a victor off a better pace; the winner was widely quoted for the 2018 Champion Hurdle afterwards, but he makes very limited appeal on that score, the list of Triumph Hurdle winners this century to make an impact in the Champion beginning and just about ending with Katchit. **Defi du Seuil** confirmed his status as the best juvenile around, winning convincingly, despite the run of the race not being conducive to him stamping his authority on things; held up, travelled well, headway fifth, disputed 2 out, led before last, kept on well run-in, ridden out; he'll be the one to beat in the Anniversary Hurdle at Aintree, and he has the physique and pedigree to think he has a longer-term future, though he has a lot of improvement to make to justify the stingy quotes for the Champion Hurdle given after the race. **Mega Fortune** confirmed himself a smart juvenile, cheekpieces again fitted, well positioned, though seeing things out so well that a greater test of stamina would surely be to his advantage; led, jumped well, travelled well, headed fifth, led again 2 out, shaken up approaching last, headed soon after, rallied run-in; he could yet have more to offer, though his future likely lies in handicaps. **Bapaume**, under less testing conditions, ran well, getting closer to the runner-up than last time, benefiting from a typically delayed challenge on this track from his rider; held up, travelled well, still plenty to do 3 out, good progress straight, went second run-in, not quicken and lost position close home; he's one of the more likely in this field to have a longer-term future. **Ex Patriot** confirmed the improvement he showed at Fairyhouse, coping with much less testing conditions, also worth bearing in mind that he got loose beforehand; dropped out, headway 2 out, chased leaders straight, disputed second jumping last, one paced; he isn't anything to look at and it may be that the best of him will be seen this spring. **Landofhopeandglory** might have been expected to benefit from being back on less testing ground but, whilst he ran creditably, he was unable to find the improvement required; held up, headway before 2 out, shaken up straight, one paced. **Charli Parcs** had looked so promising when winning at Kempton, but he's failed to repeat that form in 2 starts since, no obvious excuses for him this time; held up, effort 3 out, took closer order next, one paced straight; he could yet fulfil his early promise, though perhaps that will be as a chaser rather than a hurdler. **Coeur de Lion** ran about as well as could have been expected upped in grade, remaining with potential as his stamina is further tested; raced off the pace, ridden before 2 out, stayed on straight, bad mistake last, never landed a blow. **Landin** seemed to excel himself on his third start over hurdles, not inconceivable on his useful Flat form that he could run to a similar level in this sphere, though more likely to be flattered in running through beaten horses; raced off the pace, tailed off before 2 out, headway approaching last, stayed on. **Magie du Ma**, highly tried, ran respectably on first outing since leaving Patrick Chevillard for €210,000, in first-time hood after 9 months off; waited with, took keen hold, effort when mistake 2 out, short of room approaching last, no extra; she showed useful form when second in Group 3 company in France and ought to build on this, with mares races obviously an option next season. **Master Blueyes** failed to meet expectations, unable to confirm the improvement shown at Kempton, perhaps the different track not playing to his strengths; raced off the pace, headway when mistake 2 out, little impression straight, mistake last. **Dinaria des Obeaux**, on less testing ground than previously, was below form, seeming to find this placing insufficient emphasis on stamina; close up, led fifth, headed 2 out, outpaced straight. **Evening Hush** had been no match for Defi du Seuil in the Finale and again wasn't up to the task, that she dropped away as late as she did an indication of the way the race was run; chased leaders, bad mistake fifth, weakened approaching last. **Dandy Mag** had looked very promising at Gowran, but this was clearly a step up in grade that came much too soon in his development; raced off the pace, novicey mistakes, left behind 3 out; likely to do better, given time. **I See You Well**, on first outing since leaving John Joseph Hanlon, was out of depth; prominent, weakening when mistake 2 out. **Soldier In Action** ran poorly up in grade, one of the first in trouble, perhaps this coming too soon after just 2 starts over hurdles; in touch, ridden after fifth, weakened before 2 out.

Albert Bartlett Novices' Hurdle (Spa) (Grade 1) (1)

Pos	Btn	Horse	Age	Wgt	Eq	Trainer	Jockey	SP
1		PENHILL	6	11-5		W. P. Mullins, Ireland	P. Townend	16/1
2	3½	MONALEE (IRE)	6	11-5		Henry de Bromhead, Ireland	D. J. Mullins	8/1
3	4	WHOLESTONE (IRE)	6	11-5		Nigel Twiston-Davies	Daryl Jacob	13/2
4	8	CONSTANTINE BAY	6	11-5		Nicky Henderson	Nico de Boinville	12/1
5	6	AMI DESBOIS (FR)	7	11-5	(t)	Graeme McPherson	Kielan Woods	33/1
6	4	AUGUSTA KATE	6	10-12		W. P. Mullins, Ireland	R. Walsh	11/2
7	½	ELEGANT ESCAPE (IRE)	5	11-5		Colin Tizzard	Tom Scudamore	100/1
8	6	TOMMY RAPPER (IRE)	6	11-5		Dan Skelton	Harry Skelton	33/1
9	½	STEP BACK (IRE)	7	11-5		Mark Bradstock	Jamie Moore	100/1
10	6	C'EST JERSEY (FR)	5	11-5	(s)	W. P. Mullins, Ireland	Robbie Power	100/1
11	21	BADEN (FR)	6	11-5		Nicky Henderson	Jeremiah McGrath	100/1
F		THE WORLDS END (IRE)	6	11-5		Tom George	A. P. Heskin	10/1
ur		DEATH DUTY (IRE)	6	11-5		Gordon Elliott, Ireland	B. J. Cooper	13/8f
pu		TURCAGUA (FR)	7	11-5	(h)	W. P. Mullins, Ireland	D. E. Mullins	66/1
pu		ANY DRAMA (IRE)	6	11-5	(s)	Harry Fry	Noel Fehily	25/1

15 ran Race Time 5m 49.40 Closing Sectional (7.1f): 99.3s (104.2%) Winning Owner: Mr Tony Bloom

This looked a good renewal beforehand of the newest of the Grade 1 novices at the Festival, but it proved a rather unsatisfactory race, run at a muddling pace and not testing stamina to the same extent that it usually does, several of the more likely contenders either inconvenienced or making crucial mistakes, the form possibly not going to prove the most reliable and the winner not necessarily the best prospect in the field. **Penhill** showed yet more improvement, his Flat background an advantage under these much less testing conditions, the steady pace helping as well; dropped out, travelled well, yet to be asked for effort when hampered 2 out, good progress straight, led last, kept going well; he's done well as a novice over hurdles, but it would be a slight surprise if some of the others in the field don't turn out better longer term, with a campaign back on the Flat mentioned afterwards by connections. **Monalee** ran at least as well as previously and might have won under other circumstances, making his move ahead of the winner, which tends not to be ideal, even in a race run as this was, the better prospect of the pair so far as jumping is concerned; prominent, tanked along, led on bridle straight, headed last, kept on; has the physique to make a chaser, and could well be an RSA candidate next season. **Wholestone** wasn't quite at his best, that form shown on soft ground, but ran with credit back at 3m, just lacking the pace of the first 2 as things quickened up in the straight; in touch, travelled well, every chance straight, not quicken after last; he's had a good season as a novice hurdler and would be one for the short-list if sent for the Sefton next month. **Constantine Bay** lost his unbeaten record over hurdles, but shaped very well, the tactical nature of the race no use to him, doing well after being stopped in his tracks 2 out to finish as he did; held up, shaken up before 3 out, badly hampered next, kept on well straight, nearest at the finish; he clearly has stamina as a strong suit, looks very much a chasing type and could be ideal for the NH Chase this time next season. **Ami Desbois** has done his connections proud this winter and ran respectably, faced with another stiffish task, just not up to holding off his challengers in the closing stages; led, mistake first, headed straight, no extra before last. **Augusta Kate** didn't get the chance to confirm the marked improvement she'd been set to show last time, again a significant mistake her undoing; in rear, bad mistake eighth, not recover. **Elegant Escape** wasn't disgraced over 2f longer trip, this company essentially beyond him; prominent, not fluent 3 out, ridden next, weakened straight; he's very much a chaser on looks and should do well in novice chases next season. **Tommy Rapper** was below form over 3f longer trip, more needed in this company anyway and a blunder he made early on putting him on the back foot; raced well off the pace, bad mistake fourth, never on terms; he remains with potential, an athletic sort who should make a chaser next season. **Step Back** was thrown in at the deep end on just his second start over hurdles and seemingly ran to a fairly useful level, though there's a chance the run of the race flatters him; prominent, weakened 2 out. **C'est Jersey** was upped markedly in trip and never looked likely to get involved, faced with a stiffish task; held up, effort 2 out, made no impression. **Baden** is an underachiever and predictably found this all too hot, even over 3f longer trip; held up, pushed along after 3 out, made no impression. **The Worlds End** had made a very favourable impression in his progress through novices and looked set to play a big part in the finish until he crashed out; held up, travelled strongly, smooth headway after 3 out, every chance when fell next; it's hard to say for sure where he would have finished, but, if none the worse, he'll surely be a big player in the Sefton, while he'll make a smashing novice chaser next season. **Death Duty** seemed sure to be suited by the extra emphasis on stamina, but failed to justify his short odds, running no more than respectably when he departed late on; held up, took strong hold, headway after 3 out, jinked approaching 2 out, held when unseated last; it's possible the less testing ground was against him, though more likely that the tactical nature of the race didn't play to his strengths, and he's likely to bounce back before long, with chasing on the cards for next season. **Turcagua**, in first-time hood, failed to get back on track after being pulled up last time, beaten a long way out; held up, mistake seventh, tailed off after 3 out, pulled up. **Any Drama**, in first-time cheekpieces and over 3f longer trip, found this beyond him at such an early stage of his career, a bit too keen in the headgear for his own good; prominent, not settle fully, weakened 2 out, pulled up before last; he'd been progressing well prior to this and may yet have more to offer.

Timico Cheltenham Gold Cup Chase (Grade 1) (1)

Pos	Btn	Horse	Age	Wgt	Eq	Trainer	Jockey	SP
1		SIZING JOHN	7	11-10		Mrs J. Harrington, Ireland	Robbie Power	7/1
2	2¾	MINELLA ROCCO (IRE)	7	11-10	(s+t)	Jonjo O'Neill	Noel Fehily	18/1
3	sh	NATIVE RIVER (IRE)	7	11-10	(s)	Colin Tizzard	Richard Johnson	7/2
4	½	DJAKADAM (FR)	8	11-10		W. P. Mullins, Ireland	R. Walsh	3/1f
5	3	SAPHIR DU RHEU (FR)	8	11-10		Paul Nicholls	Sam Twiston-Davies	33/1
6	3½	MORE OF THAT (IRE)	9	11-10	(s)	Jonjo O'Neill	Aidan Coleman	14/1
7	10	BRISTOL DE MAI (FR)	6	11-10		Nigel Twiston-Davies	Daryl Jacob	16/1
8	7	SMAD PLACE (FR)	10	11-10		Alan King	Wayne Hutchinson	50/1
9	nk	CHAMPAGNE WEST (IRE)	9	11-10		Henry de Bromhead, Ireland	D. J. Mullins	14/1
10	24	OUTLANDER (IRE)	9	11-10		Gordon Elliott, Ireland	B. J. Cooper	10/1
F		CUE CARD	11	11-10	(t)	Colin Tizzard	Paddy Brennan	9/2
ur		TEA FOR TWO	8	11-10		Nick Williams	Lizzie Kelly	40/1
pu		IRISH CAVALIER (IRE)	8	11-10	(s)	Rebecca Curtis	P. Townend	66/1

13 ran   Race Time 6m 36.20   Closing Sectional (3.84f): 57.4s (100.7%)   Winning Owner: Ann & Alan Potts Partnership

A trio of 7-y-os, who had all run well in novice races at the meeting in 2016, filled the places, the winner Sizing John the youngest since 6-y-o Long Run of chasing's blue riband, his performance not in the same league as that horse, or that of Don Cossack, last season's victor, sadly now retired, but while this wasn't an outstanding Gold Cup in terms of form, it was still well up to standard and promising more, the winner only just starting to show what he can do as a stayer, the performances of the second and third the finest endorsement yet for the changes made to the NH Chase in the last decade; there were notable absentees, the King George winner Thistlecrack most obviously, though the 2015 winner Coneygree and the much lamented Many Clouds were others that would have enhanced the field; it was a race run at an even gallop, ensuring stamina came to the fore late on, the second and third both strong stayers, and it was a notably fair race, with no hard-luck stories, Cue Card falling when in touch but not going so well as others 3 out, in all likelihood the end of a notable Cheltenham Festival career which included wins in the 2010 Champion Bumper and 2013 Ryanair as well as a second to Sprinter Sacre in the Arkle. **Sizing John** has improved since stepped up in trip this year and completed a hat-trick in fine style, showing himself a top-class staying chaser, always looking to be where his rider wanted and responding really well when asked for his effort; mid-division, travelled well, effort after 3 out, led soon after next, kept on well run-in, ridden out; he'll presumably go next to Punchestown, where he ought to take all the beating, only just starting out at staying distances. **Minella Rocco**, in first-time cheekpieces, ran well, faced with his stiffest task yet, given a good ride by Noel Fehily; held up, jumped fluently, outpaced 3 out, stayed on strongly approaching last, took second dying strides; this was barely enough of a test of stamina for him and he looks made for the Grand National, obviously going to look well-in if he takes his chance, although he would be a rare 7-y-o that could cope with the demands of that race at this stage of his career. **Native River** is a splendid horse in every way and, though he came up just short in his first attempt at this level, he never stopped trying, even as others were going better than him, battling back past Djakadam near the finish; led from second, headed seventh, led again fifteenth, headed 4 out, every chance 2 out, not quicken, kept on well run-in; he was so good at Aintree last season, that he must go well in the Bowl if sent there this time, hopefully a fixture at this level for several seasons to come. **Djakadam** ran respectably in making the frame in the race for the third time—a better jump at the second last would obviously have helped but he lost third through Native River's tenacity and stamina rather than anything else; prominent, travelled well, led 4 out, strongly pressed when mistake 2 out and headed, not quicken late on; he's made the frame in all his Grade 1 chases when he's completed, but he's won only the John Durkan twice. **Saphir du Rheu** ran a cracker in the face of a stiff task, in contention until quite late in the day and sticking to his task; waited with, travelled well, headway 3 out, ridden straight, one paced approaching last; he's come back well after a disappointing season in 2015/16 and heads to Aintree in good heart, whether he tackles the Bowl or the Grand National, well-in in the latter, though his stamina not assured. **More of That** ran respectably over a slightly longer trip, not beaten for lack of stamina, just not able to get in a challenge; held up, shaken up 4 out, plugged on late on, never landed a blow; he's another that holds a Grand National entry, though, unlike others, he didn't really enhance his claims for Aintree. **Bristol de Mai**, over 2f longer trip, was reverted to being ridden prominently and, though he again failed to match his Haydock effort, he promised better than his final position suggests, going smoothly, while a serious difference of opinion with his rider at the last perhaps cost him as much as 10 lengths; chased leaders, ridden after 3 out, not quicken straight, sixth when bad mistake last. **Smad Place** was more patiently ridden than usual, but fared no better than he had in 2 previous attempts at the race, his form overall this season suggesting he's not quite so good as he was; mid-division, left behind after 3 out. **Champagne West** was ultimately below form, but he shaped rather better than he had in the Ryanair 12 months earlier, as at Gowran his jumping seeming rather more assured than previously; led until second, led again seventh, headed fifteenth, weakened 3 out. **Outlander** was a disappointment on his first start since the Lexus, one of the first in trouble; held up, labouring seventeenth, tailed off when hampered 3 out; he'll presumably get a chance at compensation at Punchestown. **Cue Card** departed at the same fence he had the previous season, though this time with a bit of work to do, going less well than several too; waited with, not clear run before sixteenth, pushed along 4 out, in touch when fell next; his Gold Cup chance has surely gone, perhaps a swansong at Aintree all that might be left. **Tea For Two**, an optimistic entrant, didn't get very far; in rear, bad mistake and unseated rider second. **Irish Cavalier** has completely lost the plot since winning the Charlie Hall in the autumn, going with no zest at all; soon behind, not always fluent, pulled up before seventeenth.

AINTREE Thursday April 6
GOOD

Betway Bowl Chase (Grade 1) (1)

Pos	Btn	Horse	Age	Wgt	Eq	Trainer	Jockey	SP
1		TEA FOR TWO	8	11-7		Nick Williams	Lizzie Kelly	10/1
2	nk	CUE CARD	11	11-7	(t)	Colin Tizzard	Paddy Brennan	2/1f
3	15	SMAD PLACE (FR)	10	11-7		Alan King	Wayne Hutchinson	10/1
4	8	ASO (FR)	7	11-7	(s)	Venetia Williams	Charlie Deutsch	14/1
5	1½	BRISTOL DE MAI (FR)	6	11-7		Nigel Twiston-Davies	Daryl Jacob	9/2
6	8	SILVINIACO CONTI (FR)	11	11-7	(b+t)	Paul Nicholls	Noel Fehily	7/1
pu		EMPIRE OF DIRT (IRE)	10	11-7	(t)	Gordon Elliott, Ireland	B. J. Cooper	10/3

7 ran Race Time 6m 24.00 Closing Sectional (3.15f): 50.4s (96.2%) Winning Owner: Mrs Jane Williams & Mr Len Jakeman

An open-looking renewal of the Bowl, with every single one of them arriving with one point or another to prove, be it their current form, ability, stamina or a combination of them all; it's hardly surprising, with that in mind, that several failed to show their form on the day but it still produced a stirring finish as Tea For Two—one of the slightly younger brigade in the field—and the multiple Grade 1-winning veteran Cue Card pulled clear at the end of a strongly-run race, the former helped by a waiting ride. **Tea For Two** barely had a race in the Gold Cup, so came here pretty fresh, and produced a career best to win his first Grade 1 in open company, admittedly up against rivals who didn't fire fully on the day and helped by a more conservative ride than the one Cue Card got; patiently ridden, jumped accurately, travelled best, took closer order after eleventh, chased leader before 3 out, led between last 2 and held on gamely; there'll be deeper, tougher Grade 1s for him to contest in 2017/18 when facing more of the up-and-comers from this season's novice ranks. **Cue Card** has had another good season, adding 2 more Grade 1s to his haul, but he isn't as outstanding as he was and was even below his recent best here, admittedly having had plenty of use made of him; never far away, went with zest, led thirteenth, ridden 3 out, headed between last 2, hung left, rallied but always just held. **Smad Place** wasn't disgraced in third but has lost his edge this season; chased leaders, ridden before 3 out, left behind between last 2. **Aso** wasn't in the same form as when third in the Ryanair last time; raced off the pace, not jump well, labouring twelfth, plugged on, never dangerous. **Bristol de Mai** looks ready for a break, giving the impression that he found this coming too soon after the Gold Cup, not going with all of his zip and finishing tired; not always fluent, led until fifth, lost place gradually, headway under pressure between 4 out and 3 out, third 2 out, no extra; he has progressed again this season, no knocking his dominant Peter Marsh win, and perhaps next season he'll be able to make a bigger impact in these top staying chases, still only a 6-y-o after all. **Silviniaco Conti** has steadily declined over the last couple of years, enthusiasm waining, and this run underlines that, specifically kept fresh for the race at a track where he has an excellent record but finishing out the back; prominent, jumped on fifth, headed thirteenth, beaten after 4 out, not persevered with once held; he was retired after the race—bringing to an end a hugely successful career in which he won 7 Grade 1 races. **Empire of Dirt** clearly wasn't 100% on the day; in rear, never travelling well, headway out wide tenth, lost touch after thirteenth, tailed off when pulled up before 3 out, lame.

Betway Aintree Hurdle (Grade 1) (1)

Pos	Btn	Horse	Age	Wgt	Eq	Trainer	Jockey	SP
1		BUVEUR D'AIR (FR)	6	11-7		Nicky Henderson	Barry Geraghty	4/9f
2	5	MY TENT OR YOURS (IRE)	10	11-7	(h)	Nicky Henderson	Aidan Coleman	8/1
3	1½	THE NEW ONE (IRE)	9	11-7		Nigel Twiston-Davies	Sam Twiston-Davies	11/2
4	11	OLD GUARD	6	11-7		Paul Nicholls	Harry Cobden	25/1
5	7	RASHAAN (IRE)	5	11-7		Colin Thomas Kidd, Ireland	Sean Flanagan	20/1
6	8	IDENTITY THIEF (IRE)	7	11-7		Henry de Bromhead, Ireland	B. J. Cooper	14/1

6 ran Race Time 4m 55.60 Closing Sectional (3.2f): 44.2s (107.0%) Winning Owner: Mr John P. McManus

Buveur d'Air set the clear standard for the 2017 Aintree Hurdle and duly followed on from Annie Power last year in completing a big-race double after Champion Hurdle success last month, comfortably accounting for a couple of the old guard, My Tent Or Yours and The New One, who'd both finished behind him at Cheltenham. **Buveur d'Air** has thrived all season, unbeaten in 5 starts over fences/hurdles, but it's since returned to timber for the big spring races that he's really taken off, showing new depths, in ability and stamina, the extra 4f no problem at all as he easily followed up his Champion Hurdle win with another smooth, top-class display; tracked pace, jumped well and travelled strongly, second on the home turn, led approaching last, eased clear; he'll continue to be hard to beat and very much sets the standard for the top hurdlers at up to this trip heading into next season. **My Tent Or Yours** was ridden with an eye on seeing the trip out (failed to stay in this race 12 months earlier) and it worked as he again ran well behind his much younger stablemate, achieving a similar rating as when chasing him home in the Champion Hurdle; dropped out, settled better than usual, hit fifth, headway 4 out, shaken up 2 out, kept on, took second flat, no impression on winner; he's still a high-class hurdler if not the easiest to win with nowadays, without a win for over 3 years and a tad disappointing when faced with much easier opportunities earlier in the season. **The New One** falls short at the top level nowadays but is still tough and consistent, this another creditable effort, and with a slightly less aggressive ride he'd have been second, understandable that he tried to get Buveur d'Air in trouble on his first try over this far; forced pace, jumped badly right from 4 out, pressed on after 3 out, headed approaching last, no extra, lost second flat. **Old Guard** faced a stiff task and ran as well as entitled to; mid-division, outpaced 4 out, plugged on. **Rashaan** found this too competitive; held up, pushed along halfway, made no impression. **Identity Thief** was back over hurdles after a spell chasing but is struggling for form at present; chased leader, mistake sixth, lost place after next, weakened.

AINTREE Friday April 7
GOOD

Betway Mildmay Novices' Chase (Grade 1) (1)

Pos	Btn	Horse	Age	Wgt	Eq	Trainer	Jockey	SP
1		MIGHT BITE (IRE)	8	11-4		Nicky Henderson	Nico de Boinville	8/13f
2	2	WHISPER (FR)	9	11-4		Nicky Henderson	Davy Russell	9/4
3	18	VIRGILIO (FR)	8	11-4	(t)	Dan Skelton	Harry Skelton	14/1
4	44	MARINERO (IRE)	8	11-4		Henry de Bromhead, Ireland	B. J. Cooper	14/1
5	25	CALETT MAD (FR)	5	11-4	(t)	Nigel Twiston-Davies	Daryl Jacob	25/1

5 ran Race Time 6m 20.40 Closing Sectional (3.15f): 47.9s (100.3%) Winning Owner: The Knot Again Partnership

Nothing could match the RSA for heart-in-mouth drama but the first 2 from there—both staying novices of the highest order—still served up another thrilling spectacle, Might Bite's winning margin bigger than it had been the month before but his air of superiority not so patent, kept straight by de Boinville and kept honest by Whisper in a far more conventional race, the other 3 making up the numbers for the Mildmay's smallest field since 2012. **Might Bite** had perhaps left more behind at Cheltenham than Whisper, no burst clear this time and no room to lapse either, but the fact he was more professional all over can only bode well for his prospects in open company, even here appearing to be doing no more than necessary as his high-class stablemate stuck to his guns, having jumped impeccably under another positive ride, threatened as he idled approaching the last before asserting in the final 50 yds; he's likely to be a sight to behold in the King George back around Kempton, scene of his Feltham agony, and it's worth noting the weak feel to the established stayers, Sizing John perfectly admirable but no Kauto Star or Denman. **Whisper** has found only a mercurial—and already borderline top-class—stablemate too strong in the 2 biggest staying novices around, running his heart out both times but just not quite at Might Bite's level, remarkable though his resurgence has been this season; there wasn't any wild errancy from his stablemate this time, but Might Bite probably wasn't at his sparkling best either and Whisper still didn't have enough to master him after giving chase from starting out on the penultimate circuit, as at Cheltenham well clear of the rest all the same and putting in a performance that would have won many a more ordinary renewal of the race. **Virgilio** ran as well as could be expected up against such a high-class pair after 3 months off, the stiffer task showing in his jumping; chased leader early, mistakes fifth, eleventh, fourteenth, left behind before straight, struggling when blundered again

2 out. **Marinero** again came up short in the jumping department, not that he'd have had a chance even with a fault-free display; patiently ridden, jumped none too fluently, shaken up before straight, held when blundered 3 out. **Calett Mad**, stepping down from the 4-miler at Cheltenham, wasn't up to the task, for ability or jumping; soon steadied, not jump well, lost touch before 4 out.

JLT Melling Chase (Grade 1) (1)

Pos	Btn	Horse	Age	Wgt	Eq	Trainer	Jockey	SP
1		FOX NORTON (FR)	7	11-7	(h)	Colin Tizzard	Robbie Power	4/1
2	6	SUB LIEUTENANT (IRE)	8	11-7	(t)	Henry de Bromhead, Ireland	B. J. Cooper	10/3f
3	11	TRAFFIC FLUIDE (FR)	7	11-7		Gary Moore	Joshua Moore	14/1
4	½	KYLEMORE LOUGH	8	11-7		Kerry Lee	Jamie Moore	16/1
5	6	GOD'S OWN (IRE)	9	11-7		Tom George	A. P. Heskin	7/2
6	1	TOP GAMBLE (IRE)	9	11-7	(t)	Kerry Lee	Davy Russell	10/1
7	8	JOSSES HILL (IRE)	9	11-7	(s)	Nicky Henderson	Nico de Boinville	15/2
8	35	UXIZANDRE (FR)	9	11-7	(v)	Alan King	Barry Geraghty	8/1
pu		ROYAL REGATTA (IRE)	9	11-7	(b+t)	Philip Hobbs	Richard Johnson	25/1

9 ran Race Time 4m 57.80 Closing Sectional (3.15f): 44.6s (105.6%) Winning Owner: Ann & Alan Potts

Un de Sceaux was an obvious absentee from this year's Melling but 9 lined up for a very competitive renewal that included 2016 winner God's Own as well as Fox Norton and Sub Lieutenant who arrived on the back of career-best performances at Cheltenham; in a truly-run race it was the latter pair that came to the fore, pulling a long way clear of a couple of very smart chasers who ran their race in third/fourth, giving every reason to take a high view of the form, this one of the performances of the season by the winner. **Fox Norton** has been a revelation this season, and he progressed a fair bit more to win his first Grade 1 in emphatic fashion, relishing the step up in trip, just as his staying-on second in the Champion Chase had suggested he might; mid-division, travelled powerfully, mistake fifth, smooth headway between 4 out and 3 out, jumped on 2 out, drew clear quickly, eased towards finish and most impressive; a further increase in trip for the King George was suggested as a possibility for next season but, as well as he was suited by this far, he is still possessed with a lot of speed and his stamina for another 4f would be suspect. **Sub Lieutenant** has developed into a top-class chaser this season and deserves the utmost credit for his consistency at a very high level, placed in 3 Grade 1s now since winning the Belfast Chase in November, beaten in them by Sizing John, Un de Sceaux and now the fast-improving Fox Norton; never far away, went with enthusiasm, led ninth, headed 2 out, kept on and gave his all but was no match for the winner; he's likely to go to Punchestown and run another big race. **Traffic Fluide** shaped similarly to last time, confirming his return to form without ever truly threatening, and although back up in trip it was the same as at Cheltenham in that he did his best work late passed tired horses; in rear, outpaced 4 out, kept on well from 2 out, took third near finish; he should stay beyond 2½m looking at this. **Kylemore Lough** was back down in trip and returned to form after 10 weeks off, right in the heat of the race throughout, shaping better than Traffic Fluide for all that he was caught by that one near the finish; chased leaders, jumped well and went with zest, close up after 4 out, one paced from 2 out, lost third only late on; this firmer ground wasn't an issue for him but he handles the mud so well that perhaps his best chance of winning a big one will be under more testing conditions. **God's Own** has a cracking record overall at the big spring meetings, successful in this race 12 months earlier, but produced a rare below-par effort this time around; held up, not always fluent, headway 3 out, weakening when jumped right last 2. **Top Gamble** was back up in trip, which was expected to suit, but ran one of his lesser races, perhaps not 100% over his Cheltenham exertions; held up, took closer order ninth, outpaced between 4 out and 3 out, left behind. **Josses Hill** thrived in the autumn but hasn't performed in Grade 1s this spring, here further below form than at Cheltenham; jumped right, led third, headed ninth, weakened after 4 out; he is probably better on a right-handed track, though. **Uxizandre**, with a visor refitted, and has gone the wrong way since his comeback in January, the problems that kept him off the track possibly telling; early mistakes, led until third, disputed again tenth, folded tamely before 3 out. **Royal Regatta** clearly wasn't 100% on the day; held up, labouring badly circuit out, pulled up, something not right.

Doom Bar Sefton Novices' Hurdle (Grade 1) (1)

Pos	Btn	Horse	Age	Wgt	Eq	Trainer	Jockey	SP
1		THE WORLDS END (IRE)	6	11-4		Tom George	A. P. Heskin	3/1
2	½	BEYOND CONCEIT (IRE)	8	11-4	(h)	Nicky Henderson	Barry Geraghty	9/1
3	sh	DEBECE	6	11-4		Tim Vaughan	Alan Johns	11/1
4	¾	CONSTANTINE BAY	6	11-4		Nicky Henderson	Nico de Boinville	11/4f
5	9	BALLYMALIN (IRE)	7	11-4		Nigel Twiston-Davies	Sam Twiston-Davies	16/1
6	8	KEEPER HILL (IRE)	6	11-4		Warren Greatrex	Gavin Sheehan	9/1
7	13	ELEGANT ESCAPE (IRE)	5	11-4		Colin Tizzard	Tom O'Brien	25/1
8	6	GET ON THE YAGER	7	11-4		Dan Skelton	Harry Skelton	10/1
9	44	TESTIFY (IRE)	6	11-4		Donald McCain	Will Kennedy	33/1
pu		WEST APPROACH	7	11-4	(t)	Colin Tizzard	Tom Scudamore	8/1
pu		MONBEG CHARMER (IRE)	6	11-4		Charlie Longsdon	Brian Hughes	18/1

11 ran Race Time 6m 05.80 Closing Sectional (3.2f): 47.4s (100.1%) Winning Owner: McNeill Family

With a quartet separated by less than a length and a half at the line this possibly isn't the hottest renewal of the Sefton in terms of the bare form, but it was a thrilling race involving a handful of very likeable, progressive types; the bunched finish isn't an indication of a muddling race as competition for the lead ensured a sound pace throughout and it was a solid test at the trip, acknowledging that drying conditions at a flat track like this will always mean there's some emphasis on speed. **The Worlds End** hadn't been asked any questions when falling 2 out at Cheltenham, a case of what might have been there, but that incident had clearly had no ill effects and he gained compensation in another Grade 1, not actually needing to better the form he'd shown in the Prestige at Haydock but proving his stamina and ability to cope with a more competitive scenario; mid-division, travelled strongly, in touch circuit out, went handy out wide 4 out, led next, hit last, held on gamely; he's shown versatility this season, winning from 19.5f up to this trip on soft and good ground, and he remains open to improvement, as a hurdler first but he's an exciting chaser for the future too. **Beyond Conceit**, who was fitted with a hood, stayed very well on the Flat and was suited by this markedly longer trip, testament to his ability with the benefit of hindsight that he ran as well he did over 2m in the Supreme (sixth), improving here, and had he jumped better in the straight he may even have won; held up, travelled fluently, good progress between 4 out and 3 out, mistakes last 2, stayed on to be nearest at the finish; he remains with potential for this sort of test over hurdles. **Debece** excelled himself up in grade and trip, and is improving all the time, impressive in a handicap when last seen but taking his form to an altogether new level here; never far away, went with enthusiasm, chased leader after 3 out, hung left approaching last, kept on, lost second near finish; he has the physique and pedigree for chasing (half-brother to Don Poli). **Constantine Bay** ran creditably in the end but looked hard work, lacking any fluency all round, a hard race at Cheltenham perhaps having taken the edge off, plus he shapes like more of an out-and-out stayer than the 3 that beat him; raced off the pace, not always fluent, went in snatches, headway 4 out, chased leaders 2 out, stuck to task; he does appeal as the sort to do at least as well over fences, an exciting novice chase prospect for 2017/18. **Ballymalin** ran about as well as could have been expected upped in grade; mid-division, tracked pace sixth, outpaced between 4 out and 3 out, held between last 2. **Keeper Hill** didn't get home on first try at around 3m, shaping better than the distance beaten suggests; in rear, headway under pressure between 4 out and 3 out, chased leaders briefly, weakened before last. **Elegant Escape** wasn't up to the task, exposed as not good enough for this level already, but he's the type to do better over fences next season; chased leaders, outpaced after 4 out, weakened after 3 out. **Get On The Yager** was found out in better company; prominent, jumped none too fluently, led after 4 out, headed next, weakened. **Testify** faced a stiff task in this grade but might have been amiss given how quickly he was beaten; prominent, led fourth, blundered 4 out, headed soon after, soon done with. **West Approach**, in first-time tongue strap, proved to be a disappointment; in rear, jumped sketchily, never travelling well, made no impression. **Monbeg Charmer** ran no sort of race; fractious at start, raced freely, led until fourth, lost place fifth, struggling badly circuit out, looked awkward.

AINTREE Saturday April 8
GOOD

Doom Bar Maghull Novices' Chase (Grade 1) (1)

Pos	Btn	Horse	Age	Wgt	Eq	Trainer	Jockey	SP
1		SAN BENEDETO (FR)	6	11-4	(s+t)	Paul Nicholls	Nick Scholfield	4/1
2	hd	FOREST BIHAN (FR)	6	11-4		Brian Ellison	Brian Hughes	6/1
3	13	CHARBEL (IRE)	6	11-4	(t)	Kim Bailey	David Bass	6/5f
4	18	COLLA PIER (IRE)	8	10-11		David Peter Dunne, Ireland	Robert Dunne	33/1
F		POLITOLOGUE (FR)	6	11-4	(h)	Paul Nicholls	Sam Twiston-Davies	5/2

5 ran Race Time 3m 56.50 Closing Sectional (3.15f): 48.1s (98.0%) Winning Owner: Mr P. J. Vogt

A race won by Sprinter Sacre, Douvan and Special Tiara in recent times, so clearly this was a substandard running to start with, and with the uneasy favourite running well below expectations it took even less winning; that was compounded by the leader stumbling and falling just after the last, which led to the runner-up stopping in front, the winner more resolute but probably really only third best on the day—he's been brilliantly placed but will do well to win a race next season. **San Benedeto**, after just 6 days off, capped a magnificent season with an unlikely Grade 1 success, essentially only third best of the trio that showed their form, but taking advantage of the situation that developed after the last; held up, ridden 3 out, not quicken next, switched approaching last, rallied to lead near finish; he'd looked likely to be difficult to place next season, that the case even more so after this, but he's a credit to himself and to connections, even if he does nothing in the future. **Forest Bihan** jumped a good deal better than he had in the Arkle, but displayed another flaw which proved his undoing after he'd effectively been gifted the race; handy, travelled well, shaken up 2 out, carried head awkwardly and not keen to go past, left in front soon after last, hesitant in front and headed close home; he clearly has questions to answer. **Charbel** looked to have a good chance of compensation for his misfortune at Cheltenham, but he was easy to back and underperformed, seemingly unnerved by a significant mistake after halfway; led, travelled and jumped well until hit seventh and headed, not nearly so fluent after, ridden 4 out, one paced, eased off. **Colla Pier** completed in her own time, a worthwhile 4 minutes work; in rear, left behind before 2 out. **Politologue** had shaped encouragingly enough in the Golden Miller and would surely have won this lesser Grade 1 but for a mishap after the last, only narrowly ahead but showing more resolution than the eventual runner-up; chased leader, took keen hold, left in front seventh, ridden 2 out, tripped and fell soon after last; he seemed to benefit from this first try at 2m over fences and that could open options for him next season.

TIMEFORM'S BEST OF 2016/17

It was time to say goodbye to some of the best horses that have lit up the jumping scene in recent seasons. Brilliant two-mile chaser Sprinter Sacre went into retirement after taking his final bow in front of his fans in the paddock at Cheltenham in the autumn, motherhood beckons for the 2016 Champion Hurdle winner Annie Power, while injury meant that Don Cossack's career highlight, the 2016 Gold Cup, turned out to be the last time he was seen in action. Another of the previous season's outstanding chasers, Vautour, was the victim of a fatal accident at home, while the demise of 2015 Grand National winner Many Clouds after a typically game victory at Cheltenham in January was another of the season's sadder farewells. But there are always new stars coming through, and the novice ranks featured some chasers who belied their experience with some prodigious feats against more seasoned rivals last season, among them Altior, who was named Timeform's Horse of the Year, King George winner Thistlecrack and Irish Grand National winner Our Duke. With the Champion Hurdle and Gold Cup titles left vacant, it was Buveur d'Air and Sizing John who claimed those crowns, though only after a change of direction for both of them; Buveur d'Air began the season in novice chases before switching back to hurdles, while a step up in trip worked wonders for Sizing John. The trainers' championships on both sides of the Irish Sea hung in the balance for much of the season, Nicky Henderson's superior Grade 1 firepower ultimately dethroning Paul Nicholls, while Willie Mullins' monopoly in Ireland came under serious threat from Gordon Elliott's increasingly powerful yard.

Staying Chasers

Colin Tizzard had the season's top staying chaser in Britain, but it was a closely-run thing between **Thistlecrack** (c174) and **Cue Card** (c173). Just two months after his chasing debut, Thistlecrack got the better of Cue Card in the King George VI Chase at Kempton, though his stable-companion was below his best in second in his bid to win it for the second year running. Cue Card had earlier won his third Betfair Chase with a fifteen-length victory over the 2015 Gold Cup winner **Coneygree** (c168), but for the second year running his own Gold Cup bid ended with a fall three out at Cheltenham. Injury ruled Thistlecrack out of the Gold Cup altogether, but not before he'd gone down narrowly to the ill-fated **Many Clouds** (c169) in the Cotswold Chase at Cheltenham. The Tizzard stable's other top staying chaser was the Hennessy Gold Cup and Welsh National winner **Native River** (c166) who was pipped for second on the line in the Gold Cup by **Minella Rocco** (c167) behind Ireland's **Sizing John** (c170).

Thistlecrack wins the King George VI Chase

In his first season with Jessica Harrington, Sizing John completed an unprecedented hat-trick of Gold Cups in the same season, winning the Irish version at Leopardstown prior to Cheltenham and then just coming out best in a thriller at Punchestown against **Djakadam** (c169), who had been fourth at Cheltenham, and Coneygree who'd been absent since the Betfair. Don Cossack's owners Gigginstown didn't have one as good as him this time, but Down Royal Champion Chase winner **Valseur Lido** (c168), Ryanair and Melling Chase runner-up **Sub Lieutenant** (c167) and Lexus Chase winner **Outlander** (c165?) weren't far behind the best around. Neither was **Tea For Two** (c166), an early casualty in the Gold Cup who then beat Cue Card in the Bowl at Aintree, while the Grand National winner **One For Arthur** (c157p) is noteworthy for still being open to improvement over fences.

Two-Mile Chasers

The immensely exciting **Douvan** (c182) was the season's highest-rated chaser but after three more bloodless victories (including an eight-length beating of Sizing John in a Grade 1 at Leopardstown) in Ireland, his unbeaten record over fences was lost in a shock defeat in the Queen Mother Champion Chase in which he finished only seventh. A sketchy round of jumping suggested all wasn't well, something confirmed when a pelvic injury later came to light. Let's hope he makes a full recovery as a clash with the latest outstanding unbeaten two-mile novice, **Altior** (c175p), would surely be the most anticipated race of the season. An Arkle winner, as Douvan was, Altior gained his two most significant wins outside novice company, beating the future Queen Mother Champion Chase runner-up **Fox Norton** (c170) in the Game Spirit at Newbury, and brushing aside the Champion Chase winner **Special Tiara** (c166) in the Celebration Chase at Sandown. Special Tiara won the Queen Mother at the fourth attempt but Fox Norton was a revelation in this division having joined the Tizzard stable, going on to win the Melling Chase at Aintree before beating **Un de Sceaux** (c169) and **God's Own** (c165) at Punchestown, the latter a winner of both those races the year before. Willie Mullins kept Douvan and Un de Sceaux apart so that the latter notched up three Grade 1 wins in Britain, beating former dual winner **Sire de Grugy** (c165) in the Tingle Creek before landing the Clarence House Chase for the second year running and then stepping up in trip for the Ryanair at the Festival.

Novice Chasers

Altior and Thistlecrack headed a high-quality crop of novices which looks sure to throw up serious challengers to the more established chasers. **Great Field** (c170p) might not have made a name for himself yet in Britain, but he won all four of his chases in Ireland for Willie Mullins, culminating in a Grade 1 success in the Ryanair Novices' Chase at

Altior (right) upsides Marracudja in the Wayward Lad

Punchestown. An exuberant front-runner, he'll be another exciting recruit to the two-mile open division. Ireland's other top novice was Sizing John's stable-companion **Our Duke** (c167p) who ran away with the Irish Grand National and looks another Gold Cup prospect for the Harrington yard. The Gold Cup is one of many possible options for **Yorkhill** (c161p) who beat the consistent **Top Notch** (c157) in the JLT at Cheltenham before losing his unbeaten record to **Road To Respect** (c156+) with a wayward performance (going right-handed) in the Ryanair Gold Cup at Fairyhouse. The latter (winner of the Plate at the Festival), along with **Disko** (c157), third in the JLT and the only horse to have beaten Our Duke over fences, make a promising pair of young chasers for Gigginstown with Noel Meade. As well as Great Field and Yorkhill, **Min** (c160P) looks another exciting chaser for Mullins. He won both his starts, including a Grade 1 at Leopardstown, before injury curtailed his season. Nicky Henderson had much the strongest team of novice chasers in Britain, the pick of them being **Might Bite** (c166) who followed up his RSA Chase win at Cheltenham with victory in the Mildmay at Aintree, beating stable-companion **Whisper** (c159) both times, though the latter almost caught him at Cheltenham when Might Bite pulled himself up on the run-in.

Staying Hurdlers

The progress shown by **Unowhatimeanharry** (h165) in novice/handicap company for Harry Fry the previous season didn't end there as he dominated the top graded events for stayers in 2016/17, this time in the colours of J. P. McManus. He had an off-day when third at odds-on for the Stayers' Hurdle at Cheltenham, but won the Long Distance Hurdle at Newbury, the Long Walk at Ascot and the Cleeve Hurdle at Cheltenham beforehand and then avenged his Festival defeat by beating Stayers' Hurdle winner **Nichols Canyon** (h165) by a head in a thrilling finish to the Champion Stayers Hurdle at Punchestown. **Yanworth** (h164) disappointed in the Champion Hurdle for McManus after being campaigned at two miles for much of the season, but, like Nichols Canyon at Cheltenham, he successfully stepped up to three miles for the first time to land the Liverpool Hurdle from the Coral Cup winner **Supasundae** (h154). **Lil Rockerfeller** (h162) failed to get his head in front, but it wasn't through want of trying, having to concede weight to Yanworth in the Ascot Hurdle and also finishing runner-up to Unowhatimeanharry in the Long Walk and to Nichols Canyon when 33/1 for the Stayers' Hurdle. **L'Ami Serge** (h161) was becoming disappointing until he was stepped up in trip, winning the Select Hurdle at Sandown on the final day of the season before going on to win the Grande Course de Haies d'Auteuil in France. L'Ami Serge had earlier finished a remote third in the National Spirit Hurdle at Fontwell behind **Camping Ground** (h166+) who ran out a wide-margin winner in soft ground on his first start for Gary Moore.

Unowhatimeanharry bounding clear in the Long Walk Hurdle at Ascot

Two-Mile Hurdlers

Yanworth might have disappointed in the Champion Hurdle after winning the Christmas Hurdle at Kempton and Kingwell at Wincanton beforehand, but J. P. McManus (and Nicky Henderson) still had the first two in the race when **Buveur d'Air** (h170), third to Altior in the Supreme twelve months earlier and winner of both his novice chases in December, proved too good for stable-companion **My Tent Or Yours** (h163), the latter finishing runner-up in a Champion Hurdle for a third time. Buveur d'Air confirmed himself a top-class hurdler when beating My Tent Or Yours along with former winner **The New One** (h158x) in the Aintree Hurdle. The latter finished fifth in the latest Champion Hurdle after registering wins in the International Hurdle at Cheltenham and Champion Hurdle Trial at Haydock for the third time. Henderson's other Champion Hurdle horse **Brain Power** (h159) disappointed at Cheltenham but had won valuable handicaps under big weights at Sandown and Ascot before the turn of the year. The Irish challenge for the Champion Hurdle was depleted by the absence of the last two winners, Faugheen and Annie Power, and it was their former stable-companion **Petit Mouchoir** (h162), now with Henry de Bromhead, who took third at Cheltenham after winning the Ryanair Hurdle and Irish Champion

Hurdle at Leopardstown. Mullins still had some high-class two-mile hurdlers to go to war with, however. **Wicklow Brave** (h161§) returned from the Flat to win the Punchestown Champion Hurdle from My Tent Or Yours and stable-companion **Arctic Fire** (h162) defied both a lengthy absence and top weight to win the County Hurdle at Cheltenham. The previous season's best juvenile **Apple's Jade** (h158) was another good hurdler Mullins had to do without, and she enjoyed a fine season for her new trainer Gordon Elliott, winning the Hatton's Grace at Fairyhouse and the top mares' races at both Cheltenham and Punchestown.

Novice Hurdlers

Labaik (h160§) was the highest-rated novice hurdler of the season but had the less enviable distinction of being one of the most temperamental too. He put his best foot forward to beat the latest Supreme hotpot from the Mullins yard, **Melon** (h150), at Cheltenham, but a reluctance to race marred much of his season and he suffered a potentially career-ending injury when fourth behind Wicklow Brave at Punchestown. Among the brightest prospects from the latest crop of novice hurdlers is **Finian's Oscar** (h150p) who missed Cheltenham but won the Mersey Novices' at Aintree and lost his unbeaten record for Colin Tizzard when edged out narrowly by **Bacardys** (h150+) at Punchestown. Besides Finian's Oscar, other good novice chasing prospects include **Willoughby Court** (h151p), who beat the ill-fated **Neon Wolf** (h152) in the Neptune at Cheltenham, and **The Worlds End** (h146p) who gained compensation for a fall at Cheltenham when winning the Sefton at Aintree in a close finish with **Beyond Conceit** (h145p) and **Debece** (h145). **Death Duty** (h148) won his first four races over hurdles in Ireland and is evidently well-regarded in the Gigginstown/Elliott camp, though he unseated at Cheltenham and was third to Bacardys at Punchestown. The same connections' **Champagne Classic** (h145), on the other hand, was successful at longer odds at both those Festivals, winning the Martin Pipe at Cheltenham and the three-mile Grade 1 novice at Punchestown, where his rivals included the first two from the Albert Barlett, **Penhill** (h152) and **Monalee** (h149), and the Pertemps Final winner **Presenting Percy** (h152). Among the juvenile hurdlers it was the Philip Hobbs-trained **Defi du Seuil** (h151p) who stood out as the winner of all seven of his starts, beating the best of the Irish four-year-olds in the Triumph Hurdle and then following up in the Anniversary Hurdle at Aintree.

SAVE £135 A YEAR!

Race Passes are the ultimate form guide, featuring ratings, all the Timeform Flags, In-Play Hints and symbols, live bookmaker prices – plus unlimited use of a 12-year archive, Horse, Trainer and Jockey Searches.

Subscriptions give you open access to Timeform data, starting from just £10 for 24 hours, to £75 for 28 days.

Why not sign-up by Direct Debit. You'll save £5 every month and get 29 free days per year. That's worth £135.

Race Passes

Ratings. Flags. Form. In-Play.
Search any horse, any race, any time.

Find out more at timeform.com and view Race Passes on the App

2016/17 STATISTICS

TRAINERS (1,2,3 earnings)		Horses	Indiv'l Wnrs	Races Won	Runs	% Strike Rate	Stakes £
1	Nicky Henderson	173	89	154	618	24.9	2,862,983
2	Paul Nicholls	161	87	171	673	25.4	2,551,969
3	Colin Tizzard	86	38	57	405	14.1	2,050,976
4	Nigel Twiston-Davies	109	55	95	586	16.2	1,581,143
5	Philip Hobbs	158	70	111	593	18.7	1,499,770
6	Alan King	128	59	104	490	21.2	1,374,407
7	Dan Skelton	202	81	118	698	16.9	1,325,478
8	Tom George	77	46	71	342	20.8	1,087,219
9	Jonjo O'Neill	156	56	78	689	11.3	1,009,134
10	W. P. Mullins, Ireland	47	7	9	52	17.3	943,394

JOCKEYS (by winners)		1st	2nd	3rd	Unpl	Total Rides	% Strike Rate
1	Richard Johnson	189	192	139	506	1026	18.4
2	Brian Hughes	144	164	128	430	866	16.6
3	Sam Twiston-Davies	137	103	91	342	673	20.4
4	Aidan Coleman	122	97	90	452	761	16.0
5	Noel Fehily	119	93	60	276	548	21.7
6	Harry Skelton	101	103	75	252	531	19.0
7	Tom Scudamore	100	100	85	469	754	13.3
8	Paddy Brennan	95	66	62	231	454	20.9
9	Daryl Jacob	87	63	53	203	406	21.4
10	Tom O'Brien	81	65	66	371	583	13.9

SIRES OF WINNERS (1,2,3 earnings)		Races Won	Runs	% Strike Rate	Stakes £
1	Kayf Tara (by Sadler's Wells)	156	982	15.9	2,188,732
2	King's Theatre (by Sadler's Wells)	113	852	13.3	2,128,480
3	Milan (by Sadler's Wells)	88	871	10.1	1,556,044
4	Presenting (by Mtoto)	124	942	13.2	1,420,119
5	Midnight Legend (by Night Shift)	121	784	15.4	1,363,552
6	Oscar (by Sadler's Wells)	96	730	13.2	1,079,414
7	Flemensfirth (by Alleged)	81	683	11.9	866,461
8	Beneficial (by Top Ville)	89	781	11.4	768,044
9	Westerner (by Danehill)	71	538	13.2	640,232
10	Authorized (by Montjeu)	44	230	19.1	604,137

LEADING HORSES (1,2,3 earnings)		Races Won	Runs	Stakes £
1	One For Arthur 8 b.g Milan – Nonnetia	3	4	610,227
2	Buveur d'Air 6 b.g Crillon – History	5	5	374,391
3	Sizing John 7 b.g Midnight Legend – La Perrotine	1	1	327,462
4	Native River 7 ch.g Indian River – Native Mo	3	5	302,548
5	Special Tiara 10 b.g Kayf Tara – Special Choice	2	5	298,141
6	Un de Sceaux 9 b.g Denham Red – Hotesse de Sceaux	3	3	296,808
7	Cue Card 11 b.g King'S Theatre – Wicked Crack	2	6	292,142
8	Fox Norton 7 b.g Lando – Natt Musik	3	5	275,700
9	Altior 7 b.g High Chaparral – Monte Solaro	6	6	262,734
10	Cause of Causes 9 b.g Dynaformer – Angel In My Heart	1	3	251,913

SECTION

THE TIMEFORM TOP 100	116
PROMISING HORSES	118
TRAINERS FOR COURSES	120
INDEX	135

THE TIMEFORM TOP 100

Hurdlers

Rating	Horse
170	Buveur d'Air
166	Camping Ground
165	Nichols Canyon
165	Unowhatimeanharry
164	Yanworth
163	Arctic Fire
163	My Tent Or Yours
162	Lil Rockerfeller
162	Petit Mouchoir
161	L'Ami Serge
161	Ptit Zig
161§	Wicklow Brave
160	Alex de Larredya
160	Diakali
160	Sutton Place
160§	Labaik
159	Footpad
158	Apple's Jade
158	Brain Power
158x	The New One
156	Silsol
155	Clondaw Warrior
155	Cole Harden
155	Finian's Oscar
155	Modus
154	Agrapart
154	Ivan Grozny
154	Shaneshill
154	Sharp Rise
154	Supasundae
154§	Renneti
153p	Campeador
153	Irving
153	Native River
153	Snow Falcon
152	Ivanovich Gorbatov
152	Penhill
152	Presenting Percy
152	Taquin du Seuil
151p	Defi du Seuil
151p	Willoughby Court
150+	Bacardys
151	Ballyoptic
151	Garde La Victoire
151	Sceau Royal
151	Vroum Vroum Mag
150	Ch'tibello
150	Limini
150	Melon
150	Thomas Hobson
150x	Hidden Cyclone
149	Monalee
149	Old Guard
149	Open Eagle
149	River Wylde
149	Seeyouatmidnight
148+	Mick Jazz
148	Chesterfield
148	Death Duty
148	Lieutenant Colonel
148	One Track Mind
148	Tombstone
147	Champagne Classic
147	De Plotting Shed
147	Jezki
147	Jury Duty
147	Messire des Obeaux
147	Mister Miyagi
147	Monksland
147	Starchitect
147	Thousand Stars
147	Volnay de Thaix
147	Who Dares Wins
147	Wholestone
147	Zarkandar
146p	The Worlds End
146	Aux Ptits Soins
146	Bapaume
146	Barney Dwan
146	Clyne
146	Diego du Charmil
146	Rashaan
145p	Beyond Conceit
145+	Aubusson
145+	Un Temps Pour Tout
145	Adrien du Pont
145	Ballyandy
145	Bamako Moriviere
145	Brother Tedd
145	Court Minstrel
145	Debece
145	Desert Cry
145	Le Rocher
145	Movewiththetimes
145	Quick Jack
145	Saturnas
145	Shelford
145	Ubak

Chasers

Rating	Horse
182	Douvan
175p	Altior
174	Thistlecrack
173	Cue Card
170p	Great Field
170	Fox Norton
170	Sizing John
169	Djakadam
169	Un de Sceaux
168	Coneygree
168	Valseur Lido
167p	Our Duke
167	Minella Rocco
167	Sub Lieutenant
166	Might Bite
166	Native River
166	Special Tiara
166	Tea For Two
165	God's Own
165	Outlander
165	Sire de Grugy
163	Don Poli
163	Empire of Dirt
162	Un Temps Pour Tout
162x	Champagne West
161p	Yorkhill
161+	Ar Mad
161	Saphir du Rheu
161	Smad Place
161	The Last Samuri
161	Zabana
161?	Alary
160P	Min
160	Aso
160	Definitly Red
160	Silviniaco Conti
160	Uxizandre
159p	Coney Island
159	Ballycasey
159	Bristol de Mai
159	Carlingford Lough
159	Garde La Victoire
159	Irish Cavalier
159	Kylemore Lough
159	More of That
159	Seeyouatmidnight
159	Sir Valentino
159	Top Gamble
159	Vaniteux
159	Village Vic
159	Whisper
158	Blaklion
158	Noble Endeavor
158	Otago Trail
158	Taquin du Seuil
157p	One For Arthur
157	Alelchi Inois
157	Devils Bride
157	Disko
157	Rock The World
157	Royal Regatta
157	Sizing Codelco
157	Sizing Granite
157	Top Notch
156p	American
156+	Road To Respect
156	Black Hercules
156	Josses Hill
156	Tenor Nivernais
156	Traffic Fluide
155p	Buveur d'Air
155	Ballynagour
155	Charbel
155	Dodging Bullets
155	Shantou Flyer
155	Vieux Lion Rouge
154	Ball d'Arc
154	Cause of Causes
154	Flying Angel
154	Lord Scoundrel
154	Simply Ned

154§	Vibrato Valtat
153	Cloudy Dream
153	Politologue
153	Roi des Francs
153	San Benedeto
153	Theatre Guide
152+	Kitten Rock
152+	Road To Riches
152	Carole's Destrier
152	Clarcam
152	Don't Touch It
152	Double Shuffle
152	Ordinary World
152	Perfect Candidate
152	Sharp Rise
152	Three Musketeers
152	Yala Enki

Juvenile Hurdlers

151p	Defi du Seuil
146	Bapaume
145	Mega Fortune
144	Charli Parcs
143	Landofhopeandglory
142	Divin Bere
141p	Call Me Lord
139p	Cliffs of Dover
139	Master Blueyes
137	Coeur de Lion
137	Ex Patriot
136p	Mengli Khan
136	Project Bluebook
135+	Meri Devie
135	Dandy Mag
134p	Bedrock
134	Dolos
134	Titi de Montmartre
133	Don Bersy
133	Flying Tiger
133	Forth Bridge
131	Soldier In Action
130	Dinaria des Obeaux
130	Magie du Ma
129	Domperignon du Lys
129	Nietzsche
128	Diable de Sivola
128	Evening Hush
128	Fidux
128	Landin

128	Monsieur Co

Novice Hurdlers

160§	Labaik
155	Finian's Oscar
152	Penhill
152	Presenting Percy
151p	Willoughby Court
150+	Bacardys
150	Melon
149	Monalee
149	River Wylde
148+	Mick Jazz
148	Death Duty
147	Champagne Classic
147	Messire des Obeaux
147	Wholestone
146p	The Worlds End
145p	Beyond Conceit
145	Ballyandy
145	Debece
145	Movewiththetimes
145	Saturnas
144p	Captain Forez
144p	The Storyteller
144+	Fountains Windfall
144	Cilaos Emery
144	Constantine Bay
143	Elgin
143	No Comment
143	Rather Be
143	West Approach

Novice Chasers

175p	Altior
174	Thistlecrack
170p	Great Field
167p	Our Duke
166	Might Bite
161p	Yorkhill
160P	Min
159p	Coney Island
159	Whisper
157	Disko
157	Top Notch
156p	American
156+	Road To Respect
155p	Buveur d'Air

155	Charbel
154	Ball d'Arc
154	Flying Angel
153	Cloudy Dream
153	Politologue
153	San Benedeto
152	Don't Touch It
152	Ordinary World
151	Anibale Fly
151	Bellshill
151	Forest Bihan
151	Label des Obeaux
151	Woodland Opera
151§	Tiger Roll
150	Baily Cloud
150	Baron Alco

NH Flat Horses

118	Fayonagh
118	Paloma Blue
116	Getabird
116	Lalor
116	Western Ryder
115p	Samcro
115	Claimantakinforgan
115+	If The Cap Fits
115	Next Destination
115	Red Jack
114	Debuchet
113	Carter McKay
113	Enniscoffey Oscar
113	Monbeg Worldwide
113	Poli Roi
113	Sam Brown
112	Peculiar Places
111p	Ballyward
111	Black Op
111	Settie Hill
110	Catwalk King
110	Ravenhill Road
109p	Canardier
109	As You Were
109	Cap Soleil
109	Cause Toujours
109	Crackerdancer
109	Daphne du Clos
109	Sam's Adventure
108	Midnight Stroll
108	Planet Nine

Hunter Chasers

148	First Lieutenant
148	Hurricane Ben
142	Foxrock
137	On His Own
137	Pacha du Polder
136	Wonderful Charm
135	Balnaslow
134	Paint The Clouds
133	Mendip Express
131	Barel of Laughs
131	Dineur
131	Monsieur Gibraltar
130	Black Thunder
129	Darwins Fox
129	On The Fringe
129	Vasco du Mee
128	Big Fella Thanks
128	Galway Jack
128	Minella For Value
128	Persian Snow
128	Toby Lerone
127p	Ask The Weatherman
127	Grand Vision
127	Pearlysteps
126	Dolatulo
126	Duke of Lucca
125	Mr Mercurial
125	Olofi
125	Simply Wings
125	Top Cat Henry

PROMISING HORSES

A p symbol is used by Timeform to denote horses we believe are capable of improvement, with a P symbol suggesting a horse is capable of much better form. Below is a list of selected British and Irish-trained horses with a p or P, listed under their current trainers.

KIM BAILEY
Chateau Robin (IRE) 6 br.g..............h94p
Laval Noir (FR) 6 b.g..............h105p
Rocky's Treasure (IRE) 6 b.g..............h129p

ENDA BOLGER, IRELAND
Stand Up And Fight (IRE) 5 b.g.....h135p

ROSE DOBBIN
Coole Hall (IRE) 5 b.g..............h115p
Doktor Glaz (FR) 7 b.g..............c103p
Minella Suite (IRE) 6 br.g..............c100p
Slanelough (IRE) 5 b.g..............h110p
Wicked Games (IRE) 6 br.m..............c88p
Witness Time (IRE) 5 b.g..............h84p

GORDON ELLIOTT, IRELAND
Baby Twig (FR) 6 b.m..............b105p
Baltazar d'Allier (FR) 6 br.g..............h143p
Campeador (FR) 5 gr.g..............h153p
Cracking Smart (FR) 5 b. or br.g..h123p
Mengli Khan (IRE) 4 b.g..............h136p
Mon Eldorado (FR) 5 b.g..............b90p
Monkshood (IRE) 5 br.g..............h117p
Samcro (IRE) 5 ch.g..............b116p
The Storyteller (IRE) 6 ch.g..............h144p
Tullyglush (IRE) 5 b.m..............h92p

BRIAN ELLISON
Bordeaux Bill (IRE) 6 b.g..............h128p
Green Light 6 b.g..............h96p

HARRY FRY
American (FR) 7 b.g..............c156p
An Siltean (IRE) 6 b.g..............h105p
Black Mischief 5 b.g..............h127p
Bullionaire (IRE) 4 b.g..............b105p
Hell's Kitchen 6 b.g..............c133P
Mountain Eagle (IRE) 8 b.g..............c111p
Outofthisworld (IRE) 4 b. or br.f.....b95P
Queen Odessa (IRE) 6 b.m..............h102p
Tangley 5 b.m..............h100p
Wotzizname (IRE) 7 b.g..............c132p

TOM GEORGE
Boyhood (IRE) 6 b.g..............h123p
Broom Tip (IRE) 5 b.g..............h98p
Forgot To Ask (IRE) 5 b.g..............b102p
The Worlds End (IRE) 6 b.g..............h146p

WARREN GREATREX
Penn Lane (IRE) 6 b.g..............h118p

MRS J. HARRINGTON, IRELAND
Our Duke (IRE) 7 b.g..............c167p

EDWARD HARTY, IRELAND
Coney Island (IRE) 6 b.g..............c159p

NICKY HENDERSON
Beyond Conceit (IRE) 8 b.g..............h145p
Brave Eagle (IRE) 5 b.g..............h123p
Burbank (IRE) 5 b.g..............h135p
Call Me Lord (FR) 4 b.g..............h142p
Christmas In April (FR) 5 b.g..............h107p
Doux Pretender (FR) 4 b.g..............b92p
Jenkins (IRE) 5 b.g..............h142p
Kayf Grace 7 b.m..............h133P
Lough Derg Farmer (IRE) 5 b.g.....h123p
One For The Guv'nr (IRE) 8 b.g.....c116p
Reigning Supreme (IRE) 6 b.g.....h128p
Scorpio Queen (IRE) 5 b.m..............h88p
Sunshade 4 b.f..............b95p
Tales of The Tweed (IRE) 5 b.g.....h132p
Thomas Campbell 5 b.g..............h138p
Wenyerreadyfreddie (IRE) 6 ch.g. h125p
William Henry (IRE) 7 b.g..............h143p

PHILIP HOBBS
Action Replay (IRE) 6 b.g..............h117p
Book Direct (IRE) 6 b.g..............h117p
Bridge of Spies (IRE) 6 ch.g..............h94p
Casterly Rock (IRE) 5 b.g..............h106p
Defi du Seuil (FR) 4 b.g..............h151p
Earth Lady 5 b.m..............h98p
Ice Cool Champs (IRE) 6 ch.g.....h117p
Jerrysback (IRE) 5 b.g..............h132P
Longtown (IRE) 6 b.g..............h119p
Majestic Touch (IRE) 6 br.g..............h114p
Mance Rayder (IRE) 4 b.g..............b93p
New Millennium (IRE) 4 b.c..............h101p
Robbin'hannon (IRE) 6 ch.g..............h138p
Saddlers Encore (IRE) 8 br.g..............c109p
Sneaky Feeling (IRE) 5 b.g..............h133p
Springtown Lake (IRE) 5 b.g..............h123p
Tricky (IRE) 8 br.g..............c83p

IAIN JARDINE
Daytripper 6 gr.m..............h104p
Zarocco 4 b.f..............b71p

MALCOLM JEFFERSON
Mayo Star (IRE) 5 b.g..............h109p
Mountain Hawk (IRE) 5 b.g..............b92p
Mount Mews (IRE) 6 b.g..............h140p
Waiting Patiently (IRE) 6 b.g..............c150p

ALAN KING
Beneagles (IRE) 5 b.g..............h126p
Chato (FR) 5 ch.g..............h85p
Cosmeapolitan 4 b.g..............h117P

DAVID...
David Cricket 5 b.g..............h88p
Inn The Bull (GER) 4 ch.g..............h100p
Lexington Law (IRE) 4 b.g..............h105p
Minella Charmer (IRE) 6 b.g..............c129p
My Khaleesi 6 b.m..............h120p

TOM LACEY
First du Charmil (FR) 5 ch.g..............h113p
Gabriel Oats 8 ch.g..............h91p
Isle of Ewe 6 b.m..............h117p
Super Sid (IRE) 5 b.g..............b77p

CHARLIE LONGSDON
Snow Leopardess 5 gr.m..............h137p

DONALD MCCAIN
Arctic Destination (IRE) 6 b.g.....h106p
Lastbutnotleast (IRE) 7 ch.m.....h128p
Our Dancing Dandy (IRE) 7 b.g... h105p
Take The Cash (IRE) 8 b.g..............c111p

GRAEME MCPHERSON
Ruby Wilde (IRE) 6 b.m..............h97p

GARY MOORE
Early du Lemo (FR) 4 gr.g..............h119p
Imari Kid (IRE) 4 b.g..............h113p
Master of Speed (IRE) 5 ch.g.....h115p

NEIL MULHOLLAND
Green Or Black (IRE) 5 gr.m..............h101p
Impulsive Star (IRE) 7 b.g..............h134p
Master Burbidge 6 b.g..............c114p
Shantou Village (IRE) 7 b.g..............c149p
Whatsthatallabout (IRE) 6 b.m... h121p

W. P. MULLINS, IRELAND
American Tom (FR) 6 b.g..............c140p
Bachasson (FR) 6 gr.g..............c147p
Ballyward (IRE) 5 b.g..............b111p
Benie des Dieux (FR) 6 b.m..............c134P
Blazer (FR) 6 ch.g..............c136p
Caro des Flos (FR) 5 b.g..............h133p
Childrens List (IRE) 7 b.g..............c138p
Come To Me (FR) 5 b.g..............b104p
Great Field (FR) 6 b.g..............c170p
Isleofhopendreams 10 b.g..............c136p
Min (FR) 6 b.g..............c160P
Ria d'Etel (FR) 5 b.m..............h131p
Voix des Tiep (FR) 5 b. or br.g.....b105p
Yorkhill (FR) 7 ch.g..............c161p

PAUL NICHOLLS
Binge Drinker (IRE) 8 b.g..............c140p
Brelan d'As (FR) 6 b.g..............h139p
Brio Conti (FR) 6 gr.g..............h140p
Cliffs of Dover 4 b.g..............h139p

Copain de Classe (FR) 5 b.g..........h132p
Coup de Pinceau (FR) 5 b.g..........h122p
Give Me A Copper (IRE) 7 ch.g...h136p
If You Say Run (IRE) 5 b.m..........b104p
Monsieur Co (FR) 4 b.g..........c121p
Ridgeway Flyer 6 b.g..........h124p
Secret Investor 5 b.g..........h125p
Topofthegame (IRE) 5 ch.g.....h138p

FERGAL O'BRIEN
Barney Dwan (IRE) 7 b.g..........c138p
Benechenko (IRE) 5 br.g..........h86p
Colin's Sister 6 b.m..........h137p
Diamond Fort (IRE) 5 ch.g.....h116p
Out of Style (IRE) 6 b.g..........b88p
Where's Cherry (IRE) 6 b.m.....h101p

JEDD O'KEEFFE
Sam Spinner 5 b.g..........h139p

JONJO O'NEILL
Big Penny (IRE) 5 b.m..........h107p
Lad of Luck (FR) 4 b.g..........b104p
Lithic (IRE) 6 b.g..........h122p
Manny Owens (IRE) 5 b. or br.g....h86p
Miss Beatrice (IRE) 5 b. or br.m.....h97p
Noble Robin (IRE) 6 b.g..........h112p
Pleasure Dome 4 b.f..........h105p
Plus One (IRE) 5 b.g..........h120p
Pop Rockstar (IRE) 5 b. or br.g....h108p
Rosie McQueen (IRE) 5 b.m.....h118p
State The Obvious (IRE) 5 ch.g...h101p
Wild Ginger 6 ch.g..........h83p

BEN PAULING
Kildisart (IRE) 5 br.g..........b101p
Willoughby Court (IRE) 6 br.g....h151p

DAVID PIPE
Dauphine Ereine (FR) 5 b.m.....c116p

Mount Haven (IRE) 7 b.g..........c105p
Mr Big Shot (IRE) 6 br.g..........h133p

NICKY RICHARDS
Booyakasha (IRE) 5 b.g..........b79p
Carry On Arcadio (IRE) 5 b.g.....b83p
Chapel Stile (IRE) 5 b.g..........h82p
Tetraites Style (IRE) 5 b.g..........h73p

LUCINDA RUSSELL
One For Arthur (IRE) 8 b.g..........c157p

OLIVER SHERWOOD
Piton Pete (IRE) 6 b.g..........h101p
Valdas Princess 5 b.m..........b78p

DAN SKELTON
Blairs Cove 5 b.g..........h130p
Captain Chaos (IRE) 6 ch.g......c133p
Captain Forez (FR) 5 b.g..........h144p
Charming Zen (FR) 5 gr.g..........h136p
Cosmos des Obeaux (FR) 5 b.g...h119p
Diese des Bieffes (FR) 4 gr.g.....b76p
Gortroe Joe (IRE) 5 b.g..........b89p
Indirocco (GER) 4 ch.g..........h116p
L'Aigle Royal (GER) 6 b.g..........c89p
Red Rising (IRE) 6 ch.g..........h125p
Return Flight 6 b.g..........c129p
Robin Roe (IRE) 6 b.g..........h140p
Rock Chick Supremo (IRE) 6 b.m...h97p
Roksana (IRE) 5 b.m..........b77p
Santo de Lune (FR) 7 gr.g..........h125p
Some Invitation (IRE) 6 b.g.....h128p
Spiritofthegames (IRE) 5 b.g.....h133p
Stick To The Plan (IRE) 5 b.g.....h117p
Welsh Shadow (IRE) 7 b.g..........c125p
Whiskey In The Jar (IRE) 5 b.g...b107p

SUE SMITH
Nomoreblackjack (IRE) 6 b.g....c130p

SANDY THOMSON
Spirit of Kayf 6 b.g..........h132p

COLIN TIZZARD
Machiato (IRE) 6 br.g..........b95p
Quiz Master (IRE) 5 b.g..........h84p
Robinsfirth (IRE) 8 b.g..........c144p
Sizing Brisbane 9 b.g..........c109p

NIGEL TWISTON-DAVIES
One Forty Seven (IRE) 5 b.g.....h119p

LUCY WADHAM
Potters Legend 7 b.g..........c141p

HARRY WHITTINGTON
Dara's Present (IRE) 6 b.g..........h109p
Emerging Force (IRE) 7 b.g..........c142p

EVAN WILLIAMS
Monbeg Oscar (IRE) 5 b.g..........h118p
Morianour (FR) 6 b. or br.g.....h114p
Oxwich Bay (IRE) 5 b.g..........h118p
Radical Archie 6 ch.g..........h100p
Sainlouis des Pres (FR) 4 b.g.....b72p
Shrewd Tactics (IRE) 6 ch.g.....c102p
Swift Crusador 6 b.g..........h111p
Theatre Stage (IRE) 5 b.g..........h94p

VENETIA WILLIAMS
Belami des Pictons (FR) 6 b.g.....c148p
Burtons Well (IRE) 8 b.g..........c137p
Cold As Ice (FR) 5 gr.g..........h96p
Du Soleil (FR) 5 ch.g..........h111p
Lady Karina 6 b.m..........h110p
Luckime (IRE) 5 gr.g..........b90p
Subcontinent (IRE) 5 b.g..........h76p
Tara Flow 7 b.m..........c107p
Top And Drop 6 b.m..........c112p
Willie Boy (IRE) 6 b.g..........c129p

TRAINERS FOR COURSES

The following statistics show the most successful trainers over the past five seasons at each of the courses that stage National Hunt racing in England, Scotland and Wales. Impact Value is expressed as a factor of a trainer's number of winners compared to those expected to occur by chance. Market Value is expressed as the factor by which the % chance of an Industry Starting Price exceeds random, as implied by field size. For example, a horse that is shorter than 3/1 in a 4-runner field will have a Market Value above 1.

AINTREE

Trainer	Wins	Runs	Strike Rate	% Rivals Beaten	P/L	Run To Form %	Impact Value	Market Value
Nicky Henderson	30	167	17.96%	55.66	17.33	23.08	1.97	1.65
Paul Nicholls	16	168	9.52%	54.84	-71.93	15.03	1.09	1.68
Nigel Twiston-Davies	13	106	12.26%	57.22	-18.18	24.46	1.36	1.43
Colin Tizzard	12	44	27.27%	63.41	111.49	38.64	2.92	1.19
Tom George	11	60	18.33%	58.35	37.12	30.00	1.93	1.57
Philip Hobbs	11	106	10.38%	52.34	-27.05	15.31	1.26	1.45
Jonjo O'Neill	10	96	10.42%	48.81	-37.95	19.29	1.17	1.42
W. P. Mullins, Ireland	10	63	15.87%	59.51	-15.15	28.57	1.99	2.01
Peter Bowen	10	92	10.87%	52.55	-42.30	19.81	1.09	1.29
Alan King	9	84	10.71%	52.28	-21.25	25.39	1.10	1.50

ASCOT

Trainer	Wins	Runs	Strike Rate	% Rivals Beaten	P/L	Run To Form %	Impact Value	Market Value
Nicky Henderson	33	149	22.15%	59.98	-34.25	36.45	1.78	1.98
Paul Nicholls	33	156	21.15%	60.79	-18.73	38.31	1.54	1.51
Philip Hobbs	17	103	16.50%	64.25	-2.39	31.62	1.37	1.40
Venetia Williams	14	87	16.09%	54.69	37.50	27.90	1.40	1.22
Harry Fry	12	42	28.57%	64.81	11.04	38.96	2.59	1.79
Alan King	11	79	13.92%	58.62	16.14	26.58	1.22	1.47
David Pipe	10	71	14.08%	54.70	-13.86	19.37	1.42	1.37
Colin Tizzard	10	61	16.39%	52.22	5.65	35.25	1.34	1.03
Charlie Longsdon	7	66	10.61%	46.96	10.50	21.88	0.94	1.15
Gary Moore	6	74	8.11%	43.68	-28.75	21.85	0.70	0.84

AYR

Trainer	Wins	Runs	Strike Rate	% Rivals Beaten	P/L	Run To Form %	Impact Value	Market Value
Lucinda Russell	37	292	12.67%	53.47	-139.27	24.82	0.90	1.16
Nicky Richards	30	140	21.43%	53.51	-35.25	32.87	1.59	1.74
N. W. Alexander	28	195	14.36%	49.55	-12.98	24.13	1.10	0.98
Donald McCain	22	111	19.82%	51.71	-45.54	28.68	1.37	1.73
Jim Goldie	17	142	11.97%	49.55	-38.46	21.59	0.94	1.09
Stuart Crawford, Ireland	16	125	12.80%	55.23	-41.38	26.86	0.97	1.26
Paul Nicholls	11	43	25.58%	55.47	32.00	32.56	2.37	1.58
James Ewart	11	104	10.58%	52.09	-38.53	20.23	0.84	1.05
Martin Todhunter	9	59	15.25%	50.72	6.48	25.88	1.14	1.05
Dan Skelton	8	33	24.24%	60.40	-2.01	36.36	1.77	1.99

BANGOR-ON-DEE

Trainer	Wins	Runs	Strike Rate	% Rivals Beaten	P/L	Run To Form %	Impact Value	Market Value
Donald McCain	60	319	18.81%	54.96	-23.45	27.03	1.26	1.46
Jonjo O'Neill	21	137	15.33%	52.21	-26.25	24.80	1.15	1.42
Rebecca Curtis	20	81	24.69%	59.75	-8.14	35.90	1.65	1.74
Alan King	16	58	27.59%	66.61	15.69	38.56	2.12	1.82
Venetia Williams	15	96	15.63%	55.51	-12.38	24.69	1.14	1.20
Charlie Longsdon	14	72	19.44%	53.28	-22.61	26.90	1.29	1.44
Warren Greatrex	13	40	32.50%	65.52	20.89	36.96	2.41	1.97
Nigel Twiston-Davies	12	64	18.75%	65.16	1.02	41.31	1.45	1.61
Nicky Henderson	12	45	26.67%	59.12	-12.15	45.35	1.92	2.63
Dan Skelton	11	49	22.45%	64.15	-7.26	40.52	1.81	1.47

CARLISLE

Trainer	Wins	Runs	Strike Rate	% Rivals Beaten	P/L	Run To Form %	Impact Value	Market Value
Donald McCain	40	205	19.51%	59.66	-59.98	28.42	1.37	1.64
Nicky Richards	18	78	23.08%	56.47	22.39	33.84	1.75	1.53
Sue Smith	16	122	13.11%	50.58	-25.04	24.19	1.00	1.19
Lucinda Russell	13	184	7.07%	49.79	-96.05	21.74	0.56	1.14
Malcolm Jefferson	11	50	22.00%	66.42	-5.63	30.40	1.67	1.56
Jonjo O'Neill	11	49	22.45%	63.50	-14.82	32.24	1.72	1.94
Maurice Barnes	10	69	14.49%	49.88	11.75	27.12	1.17	0.80
Jennie Candlish	8	72	11.11%	54.36	-34.25	19.51	0.89	1.01
Charlie Longsdon	8	30	26.67%	67.68	-14.45	35.45	1.90	2.67
Brian Ellison	8	51	15.69%	54.78	-16.85	27.39	1.25	1.70

CARTMEL

Trainer	Wins	Runs	Strike Rate	% Rivals Beaten	P/L	Run To Form %	Impact Value	Market Value
Donald McCain	26	111	23.42%	61.11	-17.86	28.83	1.69	1.78
James Moffatt	16	120	13.33%	55.10	45.75	22.01	1.11	1.05
Dianne Sayer	12	102	11.76%	51.71	-24.67	21.01	0.99	1.12
Gordon Elliott, Ireland	10	40	25.00%	67.24	-6.55	48.27	2.05	2.31
Peter Bowen	9	37	24.32%	66.33	2.13	33.11	2.09	1.90
John Quinn	6	14	42.86%	82.40	9.88	53.57	3.25	2.40
John Wade	5	23	21.74%	59.44	18.83	27.54	1.68	1.29
Jonjo O'Neill	5	18	27.78%	65.14	-1.70	33.33	2.10	2.05
Alistair Whillans	5	30	16.67%	56.95	13.50	19.23	1.47	1.23
Harriet Graham	5	33	15.15%	40.56	-12.25	20.69	1.08	1.05

CATTERICK BRIDGE

Trainer	Wins	Runs	Strike Rate	% Rivals Beaten	P/L	Run To Form %	Impact Value	Market Value
Donald McCain	37	172	21.51%	59.35	-18.75	34.01	1.59	1.57
Sue Smith	25	99	25.25%	61.46	59.59	37.16	2.06	1.36
Brian Ellison	18	73	24.66%	66.52	-19.32	38.31	1.95	2.02
John Ferguson	12	19	63.16%	83.13	16.38	75.00	5.17	3.48
Micky Hammond	11	150	7.33%	48.05	-80.50	16.77	0.64	0.81
Jonjo O'Neill	9	35	25.71%	58.59	0.91	40.71	1.71	1.63
Kenneth Slack	7	26	26.92%	70.89	12.00	46.15	2.27	2.03
Dan Skelton	6	19	31.58%	65.87	-1.78	42.11	2.03	2.46
Malcolm Jefferson	6	39	15.38%	57.61	-1.50	29.74	1.26	1.32
John Wade	6	43	13.95%	48.87	-19.71	25.58	1.24	0.98

CHELTENHAM

Trainer	Wins	Runs	Strike Rate	% Rivals Beaten	P/L	Run To Form %	Impact Value	Market Value
Paul Nicholls	52	422	12.32%	55.28	-11.04	27.62	1.27	1.57
Nicky Henderson	39	390	10.00%	55.95	-178.94	24.56	1.18	1.65
Philip Hobbs	36	269	13.38%	57.02	-31.53	26.79	1.59	1.54
W. P. Mullins, Ireland	33	261	12.64%	57.58	-62.91	28.80	1.82	2.00
Nigel Twiston-Davies	29	258	11.24%	51.72	-86.32	25.40	1.20	1.27
David Pipe	28	256	10.94%	50.20	-10.97	19.90	1.36	1.54
Jonjo O'Neill	22	208	10.58%	49.70	-6.04	20.67	1.39	1.37
Alan King	18	192	9.38%	54.00	-30.04	28.23	1.09	1.24
Gordon Elliott, Ireland	15	125	12.00%	59.79	34.63	28.80	1.77	1.70
Colin Tizzard	14	183	7.65%	50.44	-62.56	21.46	0.85	1.10

CHEPSTOW

Trainer	Wins	Runs	Strike Rate	% Rivals Beaten	P/L	Run To Form %	Impact Value	Market Value
Philip Hobbs	32	154	20.78%	63.39	-18.04	34.06	1.93	1.98
Paul Nicholls	26	149	17.45%	57.78	-66.67	28.05	1.51	2.33
Evan Williams	24	172	13.95%	53.04	3.28	24.58	1.18	1.24
Peter Bowen	20	111	18.02%	52.85	29.23	29.88	1.77	1.19
Rebecca Curtis	18	134	13.43%	59.11	-42.81	28.10	1.17	1.86
David Pipe	18	112	16.07%	57.69	-26.96	24.38	1.57	1.65
Venetia Williams	16	110	14.55%	57.17	-21.48	27.67	1.22	1.30
Jonjo O'Neill	16	123	13.01%	52.39	-30.71	21.92	1.31	1.41
Nigel Twiston-Davies	16	111	14.41%	55.10	-11.21	24.59	1.42	1.32
Tom George	15	67	22.39%	56.87	-15.19	30.80	1.90	1.61

DONCASTER

Trainer	Wins	Runs	Strike Rate	% Rivals Beaten	P/L	Run To Form %	Impact Value	Market Value
Nicky Henderson	38	101	37.62%	72.28	43.71	62.58	2.91	2.72
Alan King	23	110	20.91%	61.74	20.27	34.22	1.80	1.72
Paul Nicholls	19	76	25.00%	56.33	-17.62	36.70	1.67	2.01
Emma Lavelle	11	34	32.35%	57.76	10.33	35.29	3.30	1.93
John Ferguson	11	38	28.95%	67.80	3.73	45.61	2.37	3.00
Kim Bailey	10	56	17.86%	57.40	4.73	32.90	1.59	1.64
Jonjo O'Neill	9	90	10.00%	51.72	-30.84	13.62	1.04	1.23
Harry Fry	9	26	34.62%	60.56	3.54	46.15	2.38	1.86
John Quinn	9	26	34.62%	63.49	26.25	48.56	2.86	1.54
Ben Pauling	8	33	24.24%	50.99	10.40	30.30	2.17	1.46

EXETER

Trainer	Wins	Runs	Strike Rate	% Rivals Beaten	P/L	Run To Form %	Impact Value	Market Value
Philip Hobbs	43	230	18.70%	60.74	-67.02	34.73	1.57	1.97
Paul Nicholls	43	139	30.94%	67.92	-18.40	44.95	2.12	2.88
David Pipe	29	204	14.22%	53.46	-56.41	23.84	1.29	1.50
Harry Fry	25	67	37.31%	75.80	48.28	59.33	3.52	2.60
Colin Tizzard	24	157	15.29%	58.90	-47.82	25.36	1.31	1.42
Venetia Williams	17	86	19.77%	54.75	23.71	29.37	1.61	1.35
Susan Gardner	16	124	12.90%	48.21	2.21	20.09	1.21	0.93
Alan King	16	84	19.05%	62.01	-15.86	36.34	1.65	1.66
Victor Dartnall	13	107	12.15%	53.37	-37.75	26.13	1.12	1.26
Chris Down	10	110	9.09%	50.54	-24.75	19.42	0.80	0.85

TRAINERS FOR COURSES

FAKENHAM

Trainer	Wins	Runs	Strike Rate	% Rivals Beaten	P/L	Run To Form %	Impact Value	Market Value
Lucy Wadham	19	69	27.54%	63.27	28.45	40.19	1.90	1.52
Nicky Henderson	15	36	41.67%	71.71	-4.70	44.44	2.69	2.78
Neil Mulholland	15	46	32.61%	60.05	19.26	45.65	2.13	1.54
Dan Skelton	13	45	28.89%	64.28	-2.29	40.00	1.69	1.94
Tim Vaughan	10	65	15.38%	48.02	-35.72	20.43	1.00	1.37
Neil King	10	72	13.89%	53.20	1.98	15.42	0.89	0.98
David Pipe	9	19	47.37%	76.81	9.22	53.95	2.54	2.13
Peter Bowen	9	28	32.14%	69.44	9.95	39.29	2.12	1.71
Alex Hales	7	49	14.29%	54.61	-4.27	24.49	1.00	1.14
Paul Nicholls	7	20	35.00%	63.47	-1.20	40.00	1.84	2.19

FFOS LAS

Trainer	Wins	Runs	Strike Rate	% Rivals Beaten	P/L	Run To Form %	Impact Value	Market Value
Peter Bowen	52	308	16.88%	57.19	-52.10	30.72	1.23	1.18
Rebecca Curtis	50	189	26.46%	65.14	32.87	39.15	1.95	1.87
Evan Williams	41	363	11.29%	49.87	-113.26	18.60	0.81	1.10
Nigel Twiston-Davies	34	167	20.36%	56.56	4.22	31.65	1.45	1.41
Jonjo O'Neill	25	125	20.00%	56.31	-15.73	28.90	1.50	1.58
Tim Vaughan	18	193	9.33%	46.76	-108.73	15.79	0.69	1.11
David Pipe	17	116	14.66%	54.28	-38.73	25.22	1.18	1.69
Bernard Llewellyn	14	106	13.21%	48.59	69.14	20.61	0.94	0.81
Debra Hamer	13	78	16.67%	44.49	9.96	25.87	1.37	0.93
Nicky Henderson	13	36	36.11%	65.10	-6.93	53.28	2.71	3.00

FONTWELL PARK

Trainer	Wins	Runs	Strike Rate	% Rivals Beaten	P/L	Run To Form %	Impact Value	Market Value
Gary Moore	49	309	15.86%	53.70	0.58	27.27	1.24	1.31
Chris Gordon	39	274	14.23%	50.41	-7.04	21.76	1.07	1.03
Paul Nicholls	31	81	38.27%	70.11	8.76	45.72	2.16	2.12
Neil Mulholland	30	124	24.19%	57.66	10.15	33.81	1.68	1.34
Charlie Longsdon	22	95	23.16%	62.53	-15.60	38.20	1.88	1.84
Anthony Honeyball	22	76	28.95%	67.94	9.62	41.78	2.04	2.09
Philip Hobbs	15	61	24.59%	62.99	-3.91	41.23	1.79	2.01
Seamus Mullins	14	136	10.29%	47.33	-1.00	19.54	0.81	1.05
Colin Tizzard	14	88	15.91%	60.35	-34.24	32.50	1.23	1.70
Alan King	13	59	22.03%	61.55	-20.19	34.38	1.73	2.22

HAYDOCK PARK

Trainer	Wins	Runs	Strike Rate	% Rivals Beaten	P/L	Run To Form %	Impact Value	Market Value
Donald McCain	18	109	16.51%	50.76	-21.01	32.29	1.33	1.27
Paul Nicholls	17	75	22.67%	65.29	-9.62	34.50	1.62	1.78
Venetia Williams	15	92	16.30%	50.79	-10.05	21.74	1.41	1.33
Nigel Twiston-Davies	15	90	16.67%	60.27	-17.30	32.35	1.56	1.34
David Pipe	13	81	16.05%	56.66	39.00	28.40	1.73	1.43
Lucinda Russell	11	75	14.67%	44.62	31.33	18.67	1.22	0.87
Sue Smith	11	111	9.91%	56.20	3.70	26.30	0.81	1.14
Tom George	10	42	23.81%	55.35	18.75	27.25	2.24	1.55
Philip Hobbs	9	71	12.68%	55.60	-19.25	30.99	1.20	1.60
Alan King	8	47	17.02%	58.60	7.94	29.22	1.55	1.35

HEREFORD

Trainer	Wins	Runs	Strike Rate	% Rivals Beaten	P/L	Run To Form %	Impact Value	Market Value
Martin Keighley	6	15	40.00%	81.48	40.73	50.00	3.65	1.50
Nigel Twiston-Davies	6	26	23.08%	55.50	-1.75	24.15	1.90	1.47
Nicky Henderson	5	10	50.00%	70.15	4.58	66.67	4.72	3.53
Charlie Longsdon	4	18	22.22%	60.52	-5.38	22.22	1.88	2.09
Venetia Williams	4	26	15.38%	44.03	-14.65	15.38	1.41	1.68
Alan King	4	10	40.00%	75.97	14.43	50.00	3.65	2.19
Harry Fry	3	7	42.86%	78.35	5.45	85.71	3.00	2.67
Jonjo O'Neill	3	16	18.75%	55.45	16.00	31.25	2.02	1.47
Dan Skelton	3	11	27.27%	59.46	1.90	37.50	2.57	2.17
Henry Oliver	3	12	25.00%	57.45	11.50	50.00	2.37	1.21

HEXHAM

Trainer	Wins	Runs	Strike Rate	% Rivals Beaten	P/L	Run To Form %	Impact Value	Market Value
Lucinda Russell	47	241	19.50%	56.93	39.94	27.32	1.54	1.44
Sue Smith	17	112	15.18%	58.36	-25.71	28.23	1.31	1.28
Stuart Coltherd	14	65	21.54%	60.31	36.50	29.38	1.86	1.49
Brian Ellison	14	57	24.56%	62.56	11.08	30.42	1.86	1.81
Donald McCain	14	111	12.61%	51.87	-66.54	18.21	0.93	1.73
Maurice Barnes	13	96	13.54%	57.41	45.00	29.72	1.20	1.01
Nicky Richards	13	39	33.33%	61.87	22.06	38.46	2.83	1.80
Malcolm Jefferson	13	51	25.49%	73.84	-9.00	40.05	2.02	2.57
James Ewart	12	53	22.64%	55.35	9.63	27.06	1.99	1.40
George Bewley	10	57	17.54%	51.15	25.25	25.04	1.52	0.94

TRAINERS FOR COURSES

HUNTINGDON

Trainer	Wins	Runs	Strike Rate	% Rivals Beaten	P/L	Run To Form %	Impact Value	Market Value
Nicky Henderson	31	90	34.44%	70.76	-8.80	47.04	2.73	2.66
Jonjo O'Neill	28	113	24.78%	59.29	5.62	32.95	2.08	1.61
Alan King	26	111	23.42%	64.00	-11.88	43.28	1.86	2.17
Kim Bailey	19	81	23.46%	54.71	41.98	40.99	1.94	1.19
John Ferguson	19	55	34.55%	75.91	2.55	46.88	2.78	3.10
Gary Moore	16	93	17.20%	52.72	25.71	27.96	1.38	1.30
Dan Skelton	16	92	17.39%	59.29	-41.38	31.69	1.31	1.59
Charlie Longsdon	16	97	16.49%	50.80	-14.40	29.62	1.26	1.46
Venetia Williams	10	63	15.87%	56.69	-25.09	30.59	1.25	1.48
Ian Williams	9	58	15.52%	53.43	2.75	26.70	1.31	1.00

KELSO

Trainer	Wins	Runs	Strike Rate	% Rivals Beaten	P/L	Run To Form %	Impact Value	Market Value
Donald McCain	41	162	25.31%	59.42	30.12	33.00	1.92	1.91
Lucinda Russell	32	290	11.03%	52.47	-100.32	20.05	0.91	1.23
Nicky Richards	31	131	23.66%	57.38	17.44	28.60	1.86	1.72
N. W. Alexander	26	194	13.40%	49.15	0.28	22.28	1.12	1.05
James Ewart	15	95	15.79%	52.28	-5.17	23.79	1.32	1.31
Rose Dobbin	14	125	11.20%	52.44	3.50	20.37	1.01	1.01
Malcolm Jefferson	14	63	22.22%	65.17	-7.09	32.33	1.76	1.83
George Bewley	11	74	14.86%	51.07	20.50	18.16	1.31	1.15
Chris Grant	11	78	14.10%	49.73	82.63	24.32	1.22	0.93
Sandy Thomson	10	80	12.50%	56.57	42.08	28.00	1.11	1.16

KEMPTON PARK

Trainer	Wins	Runs	Strike Rate	% Rivals Beaten	P/L	Run To Form %	Impact Value	Market Value
Nicky Henderson	73	253	28.85%	64.92	41.55	39.79	2.27	2.31
Paul Nicholls	37	196	18.88%	61.67	-33.17	33.91	1.42	1.87
Alan King	28	186	15.05%	56.68	-62.03	29.65	1.30	1.62
Jonjo O'Neill	15	117	12.82%	49.89	-39.89	20.94	1.22	1.29
Harry Fry	13	61	21.31%	62.19	38.95	30.89	2.10	1.98
Tom George	12	66	18.18%	56.95	6.50	35.17	1.56	1.27
Emma Lavelle	12	76	15.79%	54.04	-6.77	33.78	1.35	1.45
Philip Hobbs	11	111	9.91%	55.96	-66.28	21.26	0.90	1.48
Charlie Longsdon	11	71	15.49%	51.67	-0.63	26.76	1.40	1.40
Colin Tizzard	10	75	13.33%	57.49	0.98	24.15	1.08	1.15

LEICESTER

Trainer	Wins	Runs	Strike Rate	% Rivals Beaten	P/L	Run To Form %	Impact Value	Market Value
Tom George	18	48	37.50%	69.24	31.75	54.27	2.63	1.64
Nigel Twiston-Davies	18	78	23.08%	57.63	13.65	30.67	1.66	1.37
David Pipe	13	32	40.63%	66.73	11.85	48.03	2.74	2.20
Venetia Williams	11	46	23.91%	59.86	-12.38	29.71	1.56	1.76
Caroline Bailey	10	49	20.41%	51.77	-6.71	29.27	1.43	1.01
Fergal O'Brien	7	43	16.28%	53.84	21.13	35.76	1.15	1.28
Philip Hobbs	7	21	33.33%	70.22	2.41	47.44	2.80	2.77
Jonjo O'Neill	6	57	10.53%	47.50	-36.50	19.63	0.80	1.17
Ian Williams	6	18	33.33%	64.63	-0.43	40.91	2.89	1.78
Charlie Longsdon	5	26	19.23%	50.37	0.60	30.77	1.34	1.14

LINGFIELD PARK

Trainer	Wins	Runs	Strike Rate	% Rivals Beaten	P/L	Run To Form %	Impact Value	Market Value
Gary Moore	13	95	13.68%	51.17	-12.83	26.37	1.01	1.32
Warren Greatrex	12	26	46.15%	71.41	14.48	53.85	3.21	2.41
Seamus Mullins	8	54	14.81%	50.51	49.00	16.67	1.11	0.89
Tim Vaughan	7	32	21.88%	59.00	-6.24	22.66	1.56	1.67
Chris Gordon	7	43	16.28%	54.64	-15.25	26.12	1.10	1.15
Nigel Twiston-Davies	6	27	22.22%	62.17	18.58	33.33	1.60	1.32
Nicky Henderson	6	24	25.00%	74.75	-5.51	57.14	1.82	2.93
David Pipe	5	21	23.81%	66.18	-1.63	29.52	1.90	1.96
Paul Webber	5	17	29.41%	68.06	33.75	29.41	2.54	1.66
Dan Skelton	5	11	45.45%	74.14	14.00	54.55	2.88	1.63

LUDLOW

Trainer	Wins	Runs	Strike Rate	% Rivals Beaten	P/L	Run To Form %	Impact Value	Market Value
Evan Williams	41	271	15.13%	52.65	-65.21	27.29	1.20	1.39
Nicky Henderson	29	99	29.29%	66.64	-24.01	41.14	2.53	2.88
Philip Hobbs	28	113	24.78%	63.05	-3.15	38.90	2.14	2.18
Venetia Williams	21	151	13.91%	55.40	-55.68	21.87	1.20	1.40
Nigel Twiston-Davies	20	156	12.82%	56.72	-71.26	26.81	1.09	1.41
Henry Daly	20	116	17.24%	63.98	-30.15	31.80	1.44	1.42
Dan Skelton	18	78	23.08%	61.54	-9.68	35.21	1.91	1.81
Tom George	16	80	20.00%	66.31	-11.25	32.44	1.68	1.47
Alan King	11	52	21.15%	68.40	1.97	32.42	1.77	2.12
Ian Williams	11	60	18.33%	55.65	-2.18	31.48	1.62	1.31

TRAINERS FOR COURSES

MARKET RASEN

Trainer	Wins	Runs	Strike Rate	% Rivals Beaten	P/L	Run To Form %	Impact Value	Market Value
Jonjo O'Neill	34	223	15.25%	52.73	-70.54	24.16	1.16	1.47
Charlie Longsdon	30	139	21.58%	60.18	-31.45	36.63	1.67	1.75
Brian Ellison	27	149	18.12%	51.30	12.71	28.44	1.42	1.30
Nicky Henderson	24	76	31.58%	68.53	17.83	42.07	2.48	2.36
Dan Skelton	21	84	25.00%	63.00	-1.98	35.56	1.93	1.88
Peter Bowen	18	87	20.69%	59.75	-12.41	32.53	1.71	1.67
Dr Richard Newland	18	69	26.09%	63.46	24.51	33.94	2.17	2.05
Fergal O'Brien	17	72	23.61%	58.67	56.50	36.17	1.78	1.12
Malcolm Jefferson	16	92	17.39%	59.64	11.88	32.22	1.34	1.30
John Ferguson	15	53	28.30%	70.31	1.05	41.43	2.33	2.59

MUSSELBURGH

Trainer	Wins	Runs	Strike Rate	% Rivals Beaten	P/L	Run To Form %	Impact Value	Market Value
Donald McCain	33	146	22.60%	59.71	32.44	33.80	1.64	1.58
Lucinda Russell	28	252	11.11%	50.30	-66.15	21.45	0.89	1.10
James Ewart	15	93	16.13%	51.33	1.78	26.71	1.36	1.37
Sandy Thomson	11	51	21.57%	65.43	43.30	36.05	1.78	1.48
Brian Ellison	10	125	8.00%	50.51	-70.62	15.77	0.64	1.34
John Ferguson	10	35	28.57%	67.25	1.29	36.29	2.20	2.39
Jim Goldie	8	102	7.84%	46.20	-41.59	14.17	0.70	0.82
N. W. Alexander	8	82	9.76%	46.62	-27.50	19.12	0.84	0.81
Chris Grant	8	78	10.26%	52.42	-21.00	21.58	0.85	0.84
Dianne Sayer	8	72	11.11%	50.53	-9.25	23.96	0.92	0.79

NEWBURY

Trainer	Wins	Runs	Strike Rate	% Rivals Beaten	P/L	Run To Form %	Impact Value	Market Value
Nicky Henderson	43	188	22.87%	59.38	-28.96	34.30	2.11	2.05
Paul Nicholls	32	182	17.58%	58.50	-18.00	33.35	1.37	1.70
Philip Hobbs	25	135	18.52%	58.90	111.27	31.58	1.66	1.62
Alan King	21	178	11.80%	63.03	-72.88	33.96	1.09	1.50
David Pipe	16	119	13.45%	51.85	-32.44	22.22	1.30	1.33
Harry Fry	14	53	26.42%	69.55	0.92	45.06	2.30	2.42
Venetia Williams	12	104	11.54%	50.17	-33.88	25.55	0.96	1.25
Nigel Twiston-Davies	12	105	11.43%	51.37	3.41	23.35	1.09	1.18
Warren Greatrex	11	71	15.49%	53.35	-17.00	25.74	1.40	1.21
Colin Tizzard	11	89	12.36%	56.82	-34.28	26.30	1.08	1.17

NEWCASTLE

Trainer	Wins	Runs	Strike Rate	% Rivals Beaten	P/L	Run To Form %	Impact Value	Market Value
N. W. Alexander	18	115	15.65%	50.30	-27.68	28.14	1.27	1.08
Lucinda Russell	18	150	12.00%	51.73	-39.97	21.77	0.90	1.19
Sue Smith	16	122	13.11%	55.87	-46.22	26.04	1.04	1.43
Nicky Richards	15	65	23.08%	60.43	-11.26	30.87	1.91	2.05
Donald McCain	15	102	14.71%	55.83	-23.98	31.86	1.04	1.64
Malcolm Jefferson	12	49	24.49%	68.73	-0.15	45.66	2.01	1.96
Brian Ellison	10	57	17.54%	57.68	-17.83	32.18	1.29	1.44
Keith Dalgleish	9	20	45.00%	70.40	26.88	45.00	3.74	1.54
Micky Hammond	8	64	12.50%	47.68	-7.13	29.74	0.91	0.89
Ann Hamilton	8	31	25.81%	59.53	2.82	35.48	1.59	1.28

NEWTON ABBOT

Trainer	Wins	Runs	Strike Rate	% Rivals Beaten	P/L	Run To Form %	Impact Value	Market Value
Paul Nicholls	42	138	30.43%	66.40	-31.35	40.31	1.99	2.43
Philip Hobbs	30	162	18.52%	59.43	-2.85	27.74	1.47	1.60
Evan Williams	20	121	16.53%	56.33	-30.45	25.81	1.17	1.24
Jonjo O'Neill	19	107	17.76%	52.96	-33.88	26.32	1.51	1.64
Martin Hill	16	111	14.41%	52.01	20.88	21.02	1.23	1.19
David Pipe	16	152	10.53%	49.07	-75.99	18.13	0.93	1.41
Tim Vaughan	16	108	14.81%	52.06	-32.62	22.57	1.26	1.35
Jeremy Scott	15	73	20.55%	65.94	20.10	27.13	1.80	1.47
Colin Tizzard	14	120	11.67%	54.56	-22.88	22.96	0.94	1.40
John Ferguson	14	37	37.84%	69.42	10.17	50.60	2.88	2.38

PERTH

Trainer	Wins	Runs	Strike Rate	% Rivals Beaten	P/L	Run To Form %	Impact Value	Market Value
Gordon Elliott, Ireland	68	245	27.76%	65.35	6.80	41.05	1.81	2.01
Lucinda Russell	42	419	10.02%	49.41	-121.42	21.28	0.74	1.08
Donald McCain	21	125	16.80%	54.38	-34.84	27.56	1.11	1.54
Nicky Richards	19	108	17.59%	58.62	7.00	32.15	1.48	1.27
Lisa Harrison	19	132	14.39%	50.93	9.08	27.51	1.15	0.99
Fergal O'Brien	17	63	26.98%	59.68	27.88	38.73	1.94	1.32
Nigel Twiston-Davies	17	92	18.48%	60.58	-25.14	29.19	1.51	1.85
Tim Vaughan	15	44	34.09%	69.49	18.76	40.52	2.04	1.54
David Pipe	13	28	46.43%	76.72	19.11	50.00	2.86	1.99
Stuart Crawford, Ireland	13	130	10.00%	50.89	-61.07	19.97	0.76	1.05

TRAINERS FOR COURSES

PLUMPTON

Trainer	Wins	Runs	Strike Rate	% Rivals Beaten	P/L	Run To Form %	Impact Value	Market Value
Gary Moore	46	253	18.18%	59.00	-33.52	29.28	1.34	1.56
Chris Gordon	24	157	15.29%	54.50	46.16	23.73	1.21	1.18
Alan King	18	50	36.00%	68.10	-7.03	42.03	2.54	2.60
Paul Henderson	17	70	24.29%	56.50	25.01	33.85	1.64	1.11
Suzy Smith	16	62	25.81%	62.49	81.38	37.63	2.23	1.25
David Pipe	15	55	27.27%	63.20	12.44	35.94	1.95	2.02
Anthony Honeyball	14	41	34.15%	68.61	9.14	49.07	2.44	1.83
Sheena West	13	94	13.83%	55.36	-7.08	27.71	1.14	1.07
David Bridgwater	13	68	19.12%	59.60	-21.84	28.78	1.37	1.41
Seamus Mullins	13	133	9.77%	47.55	-68.42	19.84	0.67	1.09

SANDOWN PARK

Trainer	Wins	Runs	Strike Rate	% Rivals Beaten	P/L	Run To Form %	Impact Value	Market Value
Nicky Henderson	42	159	26.42%	61.13	23.86	37.43	2.13	1.85
Paul Nicholls	29	191	15.18%	56.81	-33.41	27.46	1.13	1.55
Gary Moore	24	119	20.17%	48.67	93.48	28.75	1.55	0.98
Philip Hobbs	16	90	17.78%	58.73	-8.30	28.70	1.55	1.58
Venetia Williams	12	115	10.43%	52.50	-61.93	25.22	0.83	1.20
Alan King	11	65	16.92%	52.19	-0.29	26.15	1.42	1.42
David Pipe	9	68	13.24%	52.16	-33.47	25.63	1.34	1.57
Lucy Wadham	7	31	22.58%	62.88	10.33	35.48	2.18	1.34
Fergal O'Brien	7	21	33.33%	60.33	21.96	38.10	3.15	1.49
Jonjo O'Neill	6	65	9.23%	46.73	-37.38	17.25	0.86	1.50

SEDGEFIELD

Trainer	Wins	Runs	Strike Rate	% Rivals Beaten	P/L	Run To Form %	Impact Value	Market Value
Donald McCain	61	271	22.51%	58.21	-38.24	33.38	1.50	1.79
Malcolm Jefferson	30	107	28.04%	64.23	41.29	37.58	2.02	1.61
Brian Ellison	30	142	21.13%	59.50	-26.71	29.02	1.51	1.68
Sue Smith	27	199	13.57%	58.59	-29.85	31.04	1.01	1.36
Micky Hammond	26	184	14.13%	47.57	-34.69	19.46	1.03	0.95
Kenneth Slack	19	55	34.55%	66.19	38.58	41.67	2.64	1.82
Dianne Sayer	16	81	19.75%	51.98	6.25	24.69	1.52	1.02
Neil Mulholland	14	31	45.16%	68.96	14.19	51.61	2.81	2.08
Chris Grant	14	138	10.14%	48.75	-44.44	20.17	0.74	0.86
Joanne Foster	10	78	12.82%	43.16	-5.00	20.07	0.88	0.87

SOUTHWELL

Trainer	Wins	Runs	Strike Rate	% Rivals Beaten	P/L	Run To Form %	Impact Value	Market Value
Jonjo O'Neill	29	173	16.76%	59.50	-39.67	26.71	1.42	1.71
Charlie Longsdon	21	92	22.83%	59.40	-1.54	31.56	1.79	1.89
Caroline Bailey	20	91	21.98%	59.88	42.48	31.47	1.66	1.27
Tom George	20	58	34.48%	73.97	12.38	54.45	2.76	2.22
Dan Skelton	19	90	21.11%	66.42	-13.24	39.51	1.63	1.96
Tim Vaughan	15	96	15.63%	54.12	12.15	20.83	1.14	1.24
Kim Bailey	14	59	23.73%	64.25	25.23	38.88	1.77	1.63
Peter Bowen	13	63	20.63%	61.99	7.21	29.46	1.66	1.72
Nicky Henderson	13	56	23.21%	67.84	-18.56	36.98	1.79	2.73
Nigel Twiston-Davies	11	73	15.07%	52.45	-29.91	26.88	1.13	1.46

STRATFORD-ON-AVON

Trainer	Wins	Runs	Strike Rate	% Rivals Beaten	P/L	Run To Form %	Impact Value	Market Value
Warren Greatrex	21	56	37.50%	71.43	40.88	42.05	2.94	2.22
Tim Vaughan	20	126	15.87%	55.34	-6.30	27.04	1.35	1.28
Jonjo O'Neill	20	114	17.54%	53.58	6.44	26.17	1.47	1.45
John Ferguson	19	48	39.58%	73.91	4.88	50.36	3.34	2.85
Philip Hobbs	19	79	24.05%	58.36	26.98	29.55	1.94	1.58
Dan Skelton	15	83	18.07%	60.32	-16.45	34.41	1.39	1.61
Alan King	13	51	25.49%	71.22	11.95	33.54	2.16	1.88
Tom George	13	44	29.55%	61.36	46.78	37.07	2.25	1.69
Nigel Twiston-Davies	13	103	12.62%	55.35	-26.00	22.68	1.11	1.49
David Pipe	12	73	16.44%	56.34	-11.96	25.79	1.32	1.55

TAUNTON

Trainer	Wins	Runs	Strike Rate	% Rivals Beaten	P/L	Run To Form %	Impact Value	Market Value
Paul Nicholls	57	187	30.48%	72.89	0.76	48.02	2.29	2.55
David Pipe	24	178	13.48%	52.42	-67.52	24.16	1.23	1.47
Harry Fry	23	80	28.75%	72.55	-9.53	51.70	2.59	2.58
Philip Hobbs	22	137	16.06%	60.86	-61.76	29.36	1.46	2.01
Venetia Williams	16	77	20.78%	58.69	7.65	23.23	1.60	1.63
Evan Williams	16	101	15.84%	45.98	14.42	21.22	1.27	1.19
Colin Tizzard	13	104	12.50%	53.52	-33.00	25.36	1.07	1.28
Nicky Henderson	10	36	27.78%	64.97	-10.70	48.15	2.27	2.81
Dan Skelton	10	43	23.26%	58.13	-5.65	37.09	1.83	1.78
Alexandra Dunn	10	75	13.33%	40.70	9.25	17.59	1.21	0.86

TOWCESTER

Trainer	Wins	Runs	Strike Rate	% Rivals Beaten	P/L	Run To Form %	Impact Value	Market Value
Kim Bailey	19	78	24.36%	59.36	1.34	31.14	2.17	1.90
Fergal O'Brien	18	75	24.00%	59.36	7.88	30.98	2.07	1.81
Venetia Williams	15	68	22.06%	61.75	-13.33	24.24	1.63	1.65
Nicky Henderson	13	39	33.33%	78.67	-2.03	44.73	3.11	3.54
David Pipe	13	58	22.41%	60.96	-2.41	32.76	1.94	2.22
Ben Pauling	12	43	27.91%	56.91	47.38	32.34	2.54	1.67
Nigel Twiston-Davies	11	90	12.22%	52.88	-28.50	25.60	1.06	1.42
Alan King	11	35	31.43%	74.34	6.11	41.59	2.91	2.87
Charlie Longsdon	10	63	15.87%	61.11	-24.17	30.57	1.24	1.49
Henry Daly	9	47	19.15%	54.36	17.60	24.28	1.66	1.26

UTTOXETER

Trainer	Wins	Runs	Strike Rate	% Rivals Beaten	P/L	Run To Form %	Impact Value	Market Value
Jonjo O'Neill	35	278	12.59%	50.45	-96.81	22.31	1.14	1.70
Nigel Twiston-Davies	29	148	19.59%	60.39	10.34	30.48	1.77	1.60
David Pipe	24	141	17.02%	59.16	2.47	24.37	1.58	1.73
Tim Vaughan	23	181	12.71%	51.57	-68.81	20.79	1.10	1.37
Charlie Longsdon	23	124	18.55%	58.97	-21.75	30.85	1.68	1.83
Philip Hobbs	19	103	18.45%	59.30	-4.08	26.91	1.72	1.70
Sue Smith	19	114	16.67%	53.07	42.79	23.40	1.41	1.14
Donald McCain	19	187	10.16%	48.94	-89.18	18.88	0.83	1.42
Dr Richard Newland	17	54	31.48%	64.86	0.41	38.48	2.58	2.32
Fergal O'Brien	17	107	15.89%	60.13	0.78	28.30	1.43	1.33

WARWICK

Trainer	Wins	Runs	Strike Rate	% Rivals Beaten	P/L	Run To Form %	Impact Value	Market Value
Alan King	25	115	21.74%	67.52	-42.96	37.97	1.97	2.28
Philip Hobbs	23	94	24.47%	64.63	-6.88	39.10	2.06	2.24
Dan Skelton	21	108	19.44%	55.77	-31.76	32.02	1.58	1.74
Nigel Twiston-Davies	20	148	13.51%	53.55	-65.25	23.02	1.09	1.34
Jonjo O'Neill	18	137	13.14%	52.40	1.99	22.85	1.34	1.33
Venetia Williams	17	102	16.67%	58.18	-14.07	25.42	1.32	1.38
Charlie Longsdon	17	107	15.89%	57.26	-0.76	28.77	1.45	1.51
Nicky Henderson	14	49	28.57%	64.67	-4.85	41.00	2.32	2.15
Paul Nicholls	11	43	25.58%	65.73	-6.12	43.74	1.63	1.85
Ben Pauling	10	31	32.26%	61.18	23.25	40.32	3.55	1.57

WETHERBY

Trainer	Wins	Runs	Strike Rate	% Rivals Beaten	P/L	Run To Form %	Impact Value	Market Value
Sue Smith	34	229	14.85%	53.43	-78.65	28.83	1.22	1.31
Brian Ellison	21	121	17.36%	59.65	4.48	28.17	1.48	1.49
Dan Skelton	20	60	33.33%	66.19	14.16	45.83	2.51	1.95
Donald McCain	19	151	12.58%	49.82	-64.69	24.16	1.00	1.49
Micky Hammond	19	235	8.09%	44.56	-82.42	15.82	0.72	0.80
Jonjo O'Neill	19	94	20.21%	60.32	-23.09	33.06	1.63	1.76
Warren Greatrex	17	57	29.82%	67.47	13.12	38.54	2.29	2.49
Philip Kirby	15	115	13.04%	46.30	-12.82	19.37	1.29	0.99
Malcolm Jefferson	13	91	14.29%	53.26	-19.82	26.36	1.20	1.62
Lucinda Russell	12	117	10.26%	48.95	-32.13	21.14	0.82	1.20

WINCANTON

Trainer	Wins	Runs	Strike Rate	% Rivals Beaten	P/L	Run To Form %	Impact Value	Market Value
Paul Nicholls	92	267	34.46%	68.18	3.14	48.38	2.40	2.56
Colin Tizzard	30	233	12.88%	54.33	-53.21	23.56	1.11	1.31
Philip Hobbs	27	161	16.77%	57.29	-25.88	28.16	1.41	1.76
David Pipe	22	151	14.57%	54.54	-41.73	27.90	1.37	1.71
Harry Fry	20	94	21.28%	64.02	1.04	36.62	1.85	2.03
Venetia Williams	17	116	14.66%	59.62	-26.15	34.85	1.12	1.39
Tom George	16	71	22.54%	63.90	-2.72	30.69	1.70	1.42
Jeremy Scott	16	124	12.90%	51.05	-20.50	20.63	1.03	1.03
Alan King	14	92	15.22%	63.56	-24.61	27.12	1.27	1.92
Neil Mulholland	13	139	9.35%	52.42	-51.32	27.20	0.73	1.11

WORCESTER

Trainer	Wins	Runs	Strike Rate	% Rivals Beaten	P/L	Run To Form %	Impact Value	Market Value
Jonjo O'Neill	49	278	17.63%	56.53	-63.83	26.72	1.47	1.71
David Pipe	28	166	16.87%	56.25	-47.43	22.35	1.44	1.68
Neil Mulholland	23	121	19.01%	57.07	-4.82	32.18	1.64	1.39
Philip Hobbs	22	99	22.22%	64.62	10.35	29.82	1.79	1.80
Nigel Twiston-Davies	20	113	17.70%	57.20	2.53	28.39	1.56	1.48
Paul Nicholls	19	64	29.69%	69.19	-7.99	42.62	2.19	2.25
Nicky Henderson	19	69	27.54%	67.77	3.57	37.03	2.18	2.35
Peter Bowen	18	90	20.00%	59.28	5.13	32.66	1.81	1.83
Tim Vaughan	18	135	13.33%	53.97	-30.05	26.73	1.11	1.38
John Ferguson	16	43	37.21%	67.34	-8.20	43.29	2.74	2.75

INDEX

A

Acapella Bourgeois	48, 87
Acting Lass	4
Agrapart	95
A Hare Breath	82
Alary	93
Alpha des Obeaux	87
Altior	62, 72, 82, 109
American	5
Ami Desbois	97
And The New	90
Any Drama	98
Apple's Jade	112
Arctic Fire	112
Article Fifty	61
Aso	93, 101
Augusta Kate	98
Aurillac	87

B

Bacardys	49, 86, 112
Baden	98
Baily Cloud	92
Bakmaj	90
Balko des Flos	92
Ballyandy	81
Bally Gilbert	63
Ballymalin	105
Ballyoptic	95
Bapaume	96
Barney Dwan	6
Belami des Pictons	7
Bellshill	87
Beneagles	8
Beneficial	76
Better Getalong	90
Beyond Conceit	81, 104, 112
Billy Bronco	8
Black Op	9
Blaklion	74
Bob Ford	10
Bon Papa	86
Brain Power	84, 111
Brelade	85
Briery Belle	87
Brio Conti	10
Bristol de Mai	70, 100, 101
Bullionaire	60
Bunk Off Early	81
Burbank	85
Burtons Well	11
Buveur d'Air	71, 83, 101, 111

C

Calett Mad	103
Call Me Lord	12
Call To Order	63
Camping Ground	110
Capital Force	81
Captain Forez	13
Carter McKay	90
Cause of Causes	74
Cause Toujours	90
Celebre d'Allen	13

C'est Jersey	98
Champagne Classic	112
Champagne West	100
Charbel	83, 106
Charli Parcs	96
Cilaos Emery	81
Claimantakinforgan	14, 90
Clondaw Warrior	94
Cloudy Dream	82
Coeur de Lion	96
Cole Harden	94
Colla Pier	106
Coneygree	73, 107
Coney Island	50
Constantine Bay	15, 97, 105
Consul de Thaix	85
Copain de Classe	16
Copernicus	91
Court Cave	77
Crack Mome	81
Cue Card	69, 100, 101, 107
Cyrus Darius	84

D

Dandy Mag	96
Dans Le Vent	90
Daphne du Clos	16
Death Duty	72, 98, 112
Debece	104, 112
Debuchet	89
De Dollar Man	85
Defi du Seuil	17, 62, 72, 95, 112
Delire d'Estruval	64
Deyrann de Carjac	63
Diable de Sivola	19
Dinaria des Obeaux	96
Dingo Dollar	63
Disko	92, 110
Djakadam	73, 99, 108
Douvan	72, 73, 88, 108

E

Elegant Escape	98, 105
Elgin	19, 81
Empire of Dirt	93, 101
Evening Hush	96
Ex Patriot	96

F

Faugheen	71
Fayonagh	50, 89
Finian's Oscar	20, 72, 112
Fisherman Frank	91
Flemensfirth	77
Flying Angel	92
Footpad	83
Forest Bihan	82, 105
Forza Milan	22
Fox Norton	88, 103, 109

G

Garde La Victoire	88
Get On The Yager	105
Glaring	81

Global Citizen	63
God's Own	88, 103, 109
Great Field	51, 73, 109
Groundunderrepair	61

H

Heron Heights	87
High Bridge	81
High Chaparral	77

I

Identity Thief	102
If The Cap Fits	22
Imperial Eloquence	91
Impulsive Star	23
Irish Cavalier	100
Irish Roe	91
I See You Well	96

J

Jezki	95
Josses Hill	93, 104
Just Minded	24

K

Kayf Tara	76
Keeper Hill	85, 105
Kemboy	85
Kilcrea Vale	92
Kylemore Lough	103

L

Labaik	80, 112
L'Ami Serge	110
Landin	96
Landofhopeandglory	96
Laurium	62
Lil Rockerfeller	94, 110
Livelovelaugh	85

M

Magie du Ma	96
Magna Cartor	81
Many Clouds	107
Marinero	87, 103
Master Blueyes	96
Mega Fortune	96
Melon	71, 80, 112
Melrose Boy	60
Messire des Obeaux	85
Mick Jazz	52
Midnight Legend	77
Might Bite	69, 73, 86, 102, 110
Milan	77
Min	72, 110
Minella Awards	25
Minella Rocco	63, 73, 74, 99, 107
Minella Suite	26
Missed Approach	60
Molly The Dolly	27
Monalee	53, 97, 112
Monbeg Aquaduck	28

INDEX

Monbeg Charmer 105
Monbeg Worldwide 54
Montjeu 77
Moon Racer 84
More of That 99
Mountain Rock 90
Mount Mews 28
Mr Big Shot 30
My Mate Mark 91
My Tent Or Yours 72, 83, 101, 111

N

Native River 73, 74, 99, 107
Nelson's Touch 90
Neon Wolf 85, 112
Next Destination 90
Nichols Canyon 94, 110
Noble Endeavor 74
No Hassle Hoff 30
Not Another Muddle 31

O

Old Guard 102
Old Vic 76
One For Arthur 74, 108
O O Seven 87
Ordinary World 82
Oscar 77
Our Duke 54, 73, 110
Our Kaempfer 87
Outlander 100, 108
Overtown Express 32
Oxwich Bay 33

P

Penhill 97, 112
Perfect Harmony 90
Petit Mouchoir 83, 111
Pingshou 33, 81
Pobbles Bay 34
Poetic Rhythm 35, 85
Poker Play 64
Politologue 92, 106
Potters Legend 36
Presenting 76
Presenting Percy 55, 112

Q

Quick Grabim 91

R

Rashaan 102
River Wylde 80
Road To Respect 110
Robin The Raven 91
Royal Caviar 82
Royal Regatta 104
Royal Vacation 87

S

Saddler Maker 77
Sadler's Wells 77
Samburu Shujaa 62
Sam's Adventure 37
Sam Spinner 38
San Benedeto 105
Saphir du Rheu 99
Sceau Royal 84
Scorpion 77
Shaneshill 95
Shattered Love 85
Shivermetimbers 38
Silviniaco Conti 101
Simply Ned 89
Singlefarmpayment 39
Sire de Grugy 109
Sir Valentino 88
Sizing Granite 89
Sizing John 69, 73, 99, 107
Skipthecuddles 85
Smad Place 100, 101
Snow Falcon 94
Snow Leopardess 39
Soldier In Action 97
Some Plan 82
Special Tiara 87, 109
Steely Addition 62
Step Back 98
Sub Lieutenant 93, 103, 108
Supasundae 110

T

Tea For Two 100, 108

Testify 105
The New One 84, 102, 111
The Worlds End 98, 104, 112
Thistlecrack 69, 73, 107
Thomas Campbell 40
Three Stars 83
Tommy Rapper 98
Top Gamble 88, 104
Top Notch 91, 110
Topofthegame 41
Traffic Fluide 88, 103
Turcagua 98

U

Uncle Alastair 42
Un de Sceaux 92, 109
Unowhatimeanharry 60, 94, 110
Un Temps Pour Tout 64
Uxizandre 93, 104

V

Valseur Lido 108
Vaniteux 93
Virgilio 102

W

Walk In The Park 77
War Creation 62
Warthog 64
West Approach 95, 105
West Coast Time 90
Western Ryder 90
Whisper 86, 102, 110
Wholestone 97
Wicklow Brave 84, 112
Willie Boy 43
Willoughby Court 43, 63, 72, 85, 112

Y

Yala Enki 45
Yanworth 62, 72, 84, 110
Yorkhill 91, 110

Z

Zarkandar 95

Index To Photographers

The luckless Barney Dwan unseats jockey Paddy Brennan at Warwick
Defi du Seuil clears away in the Triumph Hurdle
Finian's Oscar is expected to take high rank amongst the novice chasers this season
Impulsive Star wins at Exeter on handicap debut
Mount Mews (second left) chases home fellow Fifty member Pingshou (right) at Aintree
Pobbles Bay (left) remains lightly raced over fences
Willoughby Court (right) fends off the ill-fated Neon Wolf in the Neptune
Yala Enki wins the Tommy Whittle Handicap Chase at Haydock
Acapella Bourgeois slips the field in the Ten Up Novices' Chase at Navan
Great Field is unbeaten in four starts over fences
Our Duke looks a prime Gold Cup contender this season
Four-time Champion Trainer Nicky Henderson
Bristol de Mai is unbeaten in two starts at Haydock Park
Neptune winner Yorkhill may switch back to hurdles this season
Thistlecrack wins the King George VI Chase
Altior (right) upsides Marracudja in the Wayward Lad
Unowhatimeanharry bounding clear in the Long Walk Hurdle at Ascot

Photographer	Page
Bill Selwyn	6
Bill Selwyn	18
Martin Lynch	21
Bill Selwyn	23
Bill Selwyn	29
Bill Selwyn	35
Bill Selwyn	44
Martin Lynch	45
Healey Racing	48
Peter Mooney	52
Peter Mooney	55
Bill Selwyn	61
Bill Selwyn	70
Bill Selwyn	71
George Selwyn	108
George Selwyn	109
George Selwyn	111